Learning Languages:

A Fast and easy guide for beginners to learn any foreign language

Free membership into the Mastermind Self Development Group!

For a limited time, you can join the Mastermind Self Development Group for free! You will receive videos and articles from top authorities in self development as well as a special group only offers on new books and training programs. There will also be a monthly member only draw that gives you a chance to win any book from your Kindle wish list!

If you sign up through this link http://www.mastermindselfdevelopment.com/specialreport specialreport you will also get a special free report on the Wheel of Life. This report will give you a visual look at your current life and then take you through a series of exercises that will help you plan what your perfect life looks like. The workbook does not end there; we then take you through a process to help you plan how to achieve that perfect life. The process is very powerful and has the potential to change your life forever. Join the group now and start to change your life!
http://www.mastermindselfdevelopment.com/specialreport

Table of Contents

Introduction

Chapter 1: Get into the mindset

Chapter 2: Break down the language

Chapter 3: Immerse Yourself

Chapter 4: Usage

Conclusion

© Copyright 2017 by Mastermind Self Development- All rights reserved.

The follow eBook is reproduced below with the goal of providing information that is as accurate and reliable as possible. Regardless, purchasing this eBook can be seen as consent to the fact that both the publisher and the author of this book are in no way experts on the topics discussed within and that any recommendations or suggestions that are made herein are for entertainment purposes only. Professionals should be consulted as needed prior to undertaking any of the action endorsed herein.

This declaration is deemed fair and valid by both the American Bar Association and the Committee of Publishers Association and is legally binding throughout the United States.

Furthermore, the transmission, duplication or reproduction of any of the following work including specific information will be considered an illegal act irrespective of if it is done electronically or in print. This extends to creating a secondary or tertiary copy of the work or a recorded copy and is only allowed with express written consent from the Publisher. All additional right reserved.

The information in the following pages is broadly considered to be a truthful and accurate account of facts and as such any inattention, use or misuse of the information in question by the reader will render any resulting actions solely under their purview. There are no scenarios in which the publisher or the original author of this work can be in any fashion deemed liable for any hardship or damages that may befall them after undertaking information described herein.

Additionally, the information in the following pages is intended only for informational purposes and should thus be thought of as universal. As befitting its nature, it is presented without assurance regarding its prolonged validity or interim quality. Trademarks that are mentioned are done without written consent and can in no way be considered an endorsement from the trademark holder.

Introduction

Congratulations on downloading Learning Languages: A Fast and easy guide for beginners to learn any foreign language and thank you for doing so.

The following chapters will discuss the best way for you to learn a brand new language - any language that you'd like to, in fact.

This whole book is based off of a technique that I've developed in quite a while of studying language. I've found that it's the method which works best with my brain in particular. The method is based around breaking down language learning into small easy to learn chunks, *understanding* the core concepts underlying each and every language that you work with, as well as emphasizing the concept of immersion.

I have a huge number of qualms with conventional language learning techniques. For a long time, the typical manner used to learn another language was to simply start from the very beginning.

Language learning is like learning anything else, and frankly, if you're trying to teach a child mathematics, you don't teach them subtraction one week and then long division the very next, because long division builds off of other concepts that you've already worked with before.

However, as a result of the information age, the language learning paradigm has dramatically shifted. It started with somewhat of a shift back in the 1990s when early forms of language learning software began to hit the market. And, certainly, one could always go to the local bookstore and pick up this or that book, and even get engrossed in various methods such as the *Pimsleur* method. If they wanted to be immersed, their options were either moving to the country of the language they wanted to learn, special ordering books (and VHS tapes after a while), or watching Spanish television if they were learning Spanish in particular.

In other words, linguistics became a rather exclusive club. Today, you can just Google "how to speak Korean" or "how to speak Danish" and go from there. Even 20 years ago, though, that was hardly an option.

So in the last 20 years, we've made astronomical strides in terms of language learning. Immersion focused learning has generally been regarded, hands down, as the best and most effective way to learn a language. There are manifold reasons to this, but the biggest is that we are born to learn language.

Think about it like this: the Earth is absolutely *full* of creatures. Different species roam everywhere. The world is littered with different animals which took different evolutionary paths and yet humans are the only ones with language. Why is this?

Well, because if we didn't have it, then frankly we'd be at the bottom of the food chain. We diverged in such a way that we had to figure out how to work together towards common goals. We had to learn how to work together and communicate. So in a sense, your brain is not only *driven* to learn more languages. It's in fact explicitly *motivated* to learn language, whether it be early on in our lives or at a later point. We are *made* to learn and speak language. Saying anything else is terribly dishonest to ourselves.

The fastest way for us to learn languages is to immerse in it as much as possible, because such a method taps into those historic and prehistoric methods of language acquisition that we had to adapt to and still have to adapt today, if not even *more* so due to the fact that society has gotten so advanced to the point that we literally cannot live without learning another language.

Because immersion is such a great way to learn a language, language-learning methods which are *centered* around immersion have actually started popping up since the advent of the information age. An example of such is the extremely popular Benny Lewis's Fluent in 3 Months program; this Irish linguistic anomaly went from a person who only spoke English to somebody who now speaks seven languages fluently and four well. There are also numerous websites and applications which aim to teach one specifically how to use various languages, or vocabulary at the very least. As you very well may have guessed, we're going to be trying to implementing those into our language learning process to some extent in a manner which we'll discuss more later.

So what exactly is this book's approach? Well, you may have bought it alongside my others, or you may have bought it as a stand-alone book. Its first purpose is to accompany my other books I've written as a means of offering you a surefire way to become an absolutely fantastic speaker of any language. However, its secondary purpose is to outline a cohesive method of language learning that will really help you to get to the bulk of the language that you wish to learn and ascend to linguistic heights that you're only daydreaming of right now.

So in that pursuit, here are the things which this book is going to attempt to do.

First, you need to get into the mindset of language learning. So many people talk about how they can't do this or that. The rest of the book will be rather technical, but learning a language - as with learning anything else - requires a lot of dedication and, indeed, confidence in your ability to perform with it.

The second thing that we're going to talk about is analyzing the key concepts of a language, recognizing its differences from your own rather than its similarities, and then indeed learning and applying the essential concepts of the language.. If you've read or will read any of my other books, you'll notice that this is indeed a rather common motif that I express regularly. In my opinion, there is nothing more necessary and paramount when you're learning a new language than having a firm grasp on the grammatical concepts underlying said language. I'll discuss in greater detail why this is absolutely necessary in chapter two.

The third thing that we're going to cover is the absolutely critical importance of immersion and how to use it to your benefit in order to build your knowledge of the language as well as your vocabulary. I heavily disagree with the academic method of teaching vocabulary to wishful language students by heaping it on them and making them memorize it for an upcoming test and then hardly using it again if it's not related to the next pertinently covered topic. But that's a grievance for another day (or another chapter, at least.)

The fourth and final thing that we're going to cover and which makes up this method in an essential manner is the importance of *usage*. Usage is the point at which a lot of the previously talked about topics come together and usage is what is actually going to teach you to speak and communicate in the language. *Usage* in some contexts will also naturally build your vocabulary as well as reinforcing some bizarre concepts which may otherwise escape you, like the conjugation of irregular verbs.

So that makes up the four points of my language learning methodology: *study* the history, *break down* the language, *immerse* yourself, and *use* what you've learned. It's very bare-bones and my presentations of these given topics haven't been as great due to the brevity with which I'm presenting them, but you've got my solemn guarantee that everything will click for you as you read this book just as it did for me.

There are plenty of books on this subject on the market, thanks again for choosing this one! Every effort was made to ensure it is full of as much useful information as possible, please enjoy!

Chapter 1: Get into the Mindset

There are two different primary mindsets to language acquisition in the world right now. There are more in other subsets, but the two most commonly encountered are the academic sort - the sort which has you sitting in a classroom, possibly all day, drilling you with vocabulary lessons and grammatical concepts in an academic context - and the immersive sort - these are the ones which are generally espoused by polyglots, so I think that taking time in order to establish how you can work within this framework is super important.

I don't think there's anything explicitly wrong with the academic manner. But I do think it has its shortcomings as a form of language pedagogy intended for simple and natural language learning.

The reason that we use classrooms in order to teach things and we teach in such book-based ways in general is that teaching the myriad lessons which are taught at an institution like so demands that one have dedicated linear study. For a great many things, this works well. Mathematics, a musical instrument, chemistry, and so forth. For linguistics, it *can* work, but it's very far detached from our natural forms of language learning.

What actually works best for linguistics, many have found - it's not a universal thing, remember, but it's just the thing which works best for the majority of people - is an *immersion* based learning experience. Or in other words, an experience where they're surrounded by the language and are practicing it not just in the context of tests and flash cards, but in the television they watch, the applications on their phone, the people that they talk to, and so on.

I've spoken to a lot of people in my life who have tried to learn this or that language. They always tell me that "I'm just not cut out for learning languages" or something like that, and it's absurd.

I'm going to be honest: the traditional methods for language learning require a certain amount of passivity. We aren't made to learn language passively. It's not something that we're created to do. And when people are sitting in classrooms learning drab vocab which may or may not be something they'll actually talk about, I can't help feel like there's a lack of proper action or motivation. Often, too, that's what will kill the person's ability to learn: an utter lack of motivation due to the fact that they couldn't care less about the thing they're learning.

Let me make this clear: language learning is *not* easy. It can be made *easier*, but it's not *easy*. Saying that you expect to learn a language in a month or with only ten minutes of practice a day is a lot like those diet pills that proclaim themselves to be some kind of snake oil that will make you shed 100 pounds in a year: it doesn't happen. Full stop. It is *possible* to learn a language very quickly - in two to three months - with absolute dedication and what actually totals out to a lot of hard work, just like it's *possible* to lose 100 pounds in a year. However, it is not a passive activity.

Language learning happens in three ways:

1) Receiving input
2) Generating output
3) Receiving feedback/correction

It's through these three alone that you're going to learn a language. The input could be anything. It could be a gigantic "For Dummies" book that walks through every step of the language for beginners, or it could be a barebones explanatory sheet that teachers the person the basics before putting them on their own.

The output happens in one way only: you personally creating the phrases from the concepts that you know and from the things that you know. This is the only way that output can happen.

Receiving feedback and correction happens through somebody more proficient in the language than you are correcting you on this topic or that of the language after hearing you speak. They could be anybody from a teacher to a pen-pal to a girlfriend who was fluent in the language. It doesn't matter, what matters is that somehow and some way you're getting it.

So with those aspects of language learning fleshed out, now what we need to settle is how we can get those. The fact is that a lot of people, and in fact a lot of traditional language learning systems, will put up a fight against these natural language learning mechanisms. But I refuse to do that.

Here are the things that I'm going to emphasize from a standpoint of your demeanor towards language learning:

- *Passion* for the language
- *Connection* to the content
- *Immersion* rather than arbitrary rote memorization
- *Confidence* in your ability to speak
- *Willingness* to go out of your comfort zone.

You need a *passion* for the language if you want to learn it. Even a fake one, if you have to conjure one up out of thin air. At the beginning, learning a language is going to be awful. You're not going to know anything, you're going to be extremely lost and confused. You have to care enough about the language that you're working with that you can just keep on going with it even through rough patches and plateaus.

You need a *connection* to the content if you genuinely want to retain it. I find that in a lot of people, the only way for them to remember something is if they find that to some degree they care about it. This doubles up on the first point by reinforcing the idea that if you care about something, you're more likely to both work hard on it and to retain it.

You need *immersion* rather than rote memorization because immersion is going to teach you to use the language everywhere and use context to figure out new words and sounds. This is how we naturally learn our first languages and it's how we can naturally learn even more if we manage to tap into that primitive "lightbulb" notion of making things click and making gears simply turn. This builds upon the first and second points because I insist that you immerse yourself in topics that you care about, and help you to seek them out.

You need *confidence* in your ability to speak. Not in your ability to speak the *language*, you're going to be awful at the language for a long time. You need to accept that. "A long time" could be any number of measures from a month to several years. You have to realize that your reinforcement and your feedback is only going to come by speaking to people you've never spoken to before in a language that you're not entirely comfortable in. By getting out of that comfort zone and getting comfortable "being wrong", as well as by accepting that you will often flub up in seemingly simple ways, you will become a better speaker of the language even faster.

Lastly, you need *willingness* to go out of your comfort zone. This is something that only you can give yourself. I can harp on how important this and that thing is all that I want, but ultimately it's up to *you* to summon the willpower to actually make something happen for yourself in the context of language learning.

You'll need to summon a lot of willpower, in fact. This method is "fast and easy", but it's most certainly *not* a timesaver. If you want to learn a language in 10 minutes per day, you should relegate yourself to barely knowing the language in 4 years' time. If you want to learn it faster, you have to accept that your entire world will be in that language now, to the extent that you can make it so, and you have to accept that you're going to be spending an hour or two working in that language, translating both to and from, and that's not even including any time that you spend talking to your tutor.

But if you follow through with this method, I can guarantee you that you'll be a great speaker of whatever language it is that you want to speak.

Chapter 2: Break Down the Language

This is the single most important part of this entire book. Regardless of how you decide to learn after this - whether you decide to go an immersive route or a more traditional route - it will help you immensely in your journey if you break down the language that you're working with as well as language in a general sense so that you better understand exactly what you're working with.

I'd liken it somewhat to building a house on uneven land. You're going to need a *solid* foundation in place, regardless of whether the house that you build on it is in the Gothic style, the Colonial style, the Tudor style, or the Southwestern style.

The foundation of your language will be built in two parts: understanding the concepts of language *in general*, which I'm going to help you with in this chapter, as well as understanding the concepts of language *specific to your own*, which is something that's going to require some time spent in personal study and reflection on the language.

You also need this foundation in order to build whatever house you're trying to build. If you try to build a house without a foundation, it's going to fall apart. And that's truer than pretty much everything for this super immersion heavy manner of learning: if you don't set aside time in order to focus in and learn these basic building blocks of the language, you will not succeed, point blank. You will be weighed down by the intermediate difficulty of the sources you'll be surrounding yourself with and you'll fail to understand a lot of the nuance involved with the language.

See, the reason this works is because language serves a single purpose among people. It came about for one reason, and one reason solely: to communicate information. And because of this, it is very good at that specific purpose. And language offers many nuances between them all in order to discuss the caveats of a basic situation. You can take a basic phrase, sure, but you can also add a lot of detail. "The boy is tossing the ball" could become "The young boy is tossing a red ball to the dog while his mother sits on the porch and smiles."

What I'm saying is that all situations have a logical conclusion based off of the things which we can deduce about it with our own senses. As a result of this, we can surmise that all language is, indeed, intended to refer to the situations which arise around us. And indeed, language *does* serve this purpose. Because language has served a common purpose, the structures that have developed are similar as well. Our cognition reduces everything to a logical ultimate which is then expressed through words even in languages which are unrelated.

Believe it or not, most languages were once upon a time more related than they are today. Due to the patterns of conquest and migration patterns, language would actually develop both outward and inward and would change great volumes as time went on. There are a lot of reasons for this. The languages which preceded the great changes are commonly referred to as "proto-languages".

The vast majority of languages in Eurasia can be traced back to Proto-Indo-European, also called PIE. This language is by far the best understood proto-language. A huge number of languages in both Europe and Asia can be traced back to this lineage of languages. When you follow this lineage back and try to understand where and why each form departs, you're involved in what is actually a super interesting study; an inquiry into the origins and history of a great portion of language.

So because of this alone, a great number of the languages that you may desire to learn are related in some way or another, down the line. Their syntax, of course, has definitely changed in some capacity or another since those days long ago, but that's just the natural march of language. The point I'm trying to make here is that those languages have concepts in common.

And the languages which aren't related in such a manner to Proto-Indo-European will still share many of these same features, just because they're simply required in order to form a rational thought or delineate any sort of idea. So what this means is that even if you want to speak something like Mandarin Chinese or Lao or Hebrew or Arabic, they'll still share these key concepts because the singular purpose of language is to make logical inferences based off of events. At some point, every language evolved from a tribe of people needing to say things like "Let's settle here" - "You need to milk the cow" - "How can we best grow this plant?" - "There are migrating bison out to the west that we can kill." And indeed, the vast differences between multiple languages sets you up for a great number of uniformities among them.

So, this means that we can separate our language learning process into a lot of smaller and more malleable chunks that you can take advantage of and utilize one at a time in order to get a sound result.

Learn the Differences

This point can't be made enough. I've already made apparent that languages are contextually very similar. This means that if you spend a lot of time learning the similarities between a language, you're going to find a lot of them. A whole lot of them.

I know this is a really easy mistake to make, because when I first embarked on my language learning adventures, I started out by Googling "what language is the easiest for a person to learn?" My desire to be worldly and bilingual conflicted heavily with the amount of work I was truly willing to put out in return for such a thing. As I'm sure is no surprise, it didn't really work out for me.

What I should have done *instead* of learning what was within my comfort zone was ignore that another language would be out of my comfort zone entirely. There's no reason to think that, because every language will be out of your comfort zone. When you're learning another language, there is no such *thing* as a comfort zone, because every language will differ from your own (though possibly in varying degrees).

This is to say that when I say to learn the differences, I don't mean at the theoretical level; you're not at all ready for that sort of thing just yet. Instead, just do a cursory review of things such as the Wikipedia article for the language. When you do this, you'll be able to see not only the history of the language but also a few things about it. There are certain terms that will scare you or confuse you at first - for example, *agglutinative,* which means nothing linguistically to English speakers because English isn't agglutinative - but there will normally be at the very least a cursory explanation of the term within parentheses, or a link to the article on that concept itself which will normally provide both an in-depth examination and cumulative overview of the topic.

Why learn the differences before you get too into the language itself? Because that's how it works. You have to be prepared for whatever you may be facing. For example, if you were wanting to learn Chinese, it'd suit you well to know essential things which cause it to differ from English. For example, it's a tone language, as opposed to English which isn't. The meaning of words in Chinese can change drastically depending upon the tone in which you say the word. A person with bad tones in China sticks out like a sore thumb, though as a Westerner you'll probably get a pass for even trying to learn their language in the first place.

In other words, you've just got to know what to expect, or else you may find yourself completely blind-sided by a language in some ways or another. This is the last thing you want. You need to know what to expect going into the language so that you're actually prepared and not scrambling when some technique presents itself.

Now with that little aspect out of it all, it's time to move onto the technical aspects: the things you need to learn before doing anything else.

Learn the Alphabet

This seems a little terse, I'm sure. But the fact is that there are a lot of languages which don't have Latin alphabets or even anything close. Let me put it this way: there are a lot of languages which you don't understand, and there are a lot of alphabets, too, that you don't understand.

I can think of several off of the top of my head.

First, there's *Cyrillic script*, which is used heavily by Russia, though also by countries which have developed in its approximate proximity. Languages which use the Cyrillic script include but are certainly not limited to Russian, Ukrainian, Mongolian, Kazakh, and Macedonian.

Then there are the Semitic scripts like Arabic and Hebrew. You need to learn these before doing anything else, however you can. This is for the simple fact that they can be convoluted and confusing, but also because a nifty feature of these scripts is that they can completely exclude vowels and leave you to just decipher a word based upon context. This is actually a really cool linguistic model based upon triconsonantal roots, but it can be very confusing as a beginner. It becomes even more confusing when you're trying to struggle with the basic alphabet on top of that. The alphabet should without a doubt be the first thing that you learn in these languages.

Then, for example, there's the Korean script *hangul*. This is a really simple script to learn and understand, especially because it was created specifically for Korean by a single guy in order to make Korean far easier to read. However, the case here is much like a less serious version of the case for semitic scripts: the vast majority of the source material that you'll be encountering and even language-teaching guides you may encounter will invariably be written to some extent in the language itself.

This method has some shortcomings, overall. I'll admit that. It doesn't work well for logographic languages. Logographic languages are languages which, as opposed to an alphabet crafted from individual graphs which all represent a singular sound consistently, have instead a unique character for every single word in the language. A beautiful example of a logographic language is Chinese, and Japanese would be another sterling example as well (aside from Katakana). For logographic languages, the only way at all to really learn the language is to practice it. The only way around this is if you decide to learn how things sound when they're Romanized and learn the Romanized version of the language at a faster rate than you're learning the logographic characters. You can base the characters that you're learning off of the words that you already know. This is the only feasible way I can imagine taking my language learning method and applying it to logographic languages, and it's possible but will certainly be difficult due to the lack of a real wealth of Romanized resources in these languages available for you to learn by.

Learn the Structure

Once you know the alphabet, you need to learn about the structure of a language. Languages are essentially composed of three different extremely basic components: subjects, objects, and verbs. There isn't a language that lacks any of these three components. I'll explain them more in a second.

English, for reference, is a subject-verb-object language. This is massively different compared to, say, Japanese, which is a subject object verb language, or

Arabic, which is a verb subject object language.

So what does this mean exactly? This refers to the order of the given parts of speech in a conventional sentence within the language.

Subjects - Subjects are the things which the sentence is based around. However, since this can be a little vague, it's better defined as the thing which ultimately controls or is the progenitor of the verb. The reason I add the progenitor clause is because in the sentence "It is nice," the subject is still *it* because the verb *is* (a conjugated form of *to be*) has to do directly with the verb *it*. *It* is existing in such a manner, so it's acceptable to say "It is", even if "it" isn't doing anything directly with the verb "is". Subjects are also called the *nominative case* should you be working with a language which has a form or noun declension.

Verbs - Verbs are the actions which are undertaken, but they can also indicate things such as an occurrence of some sort (*to become*) or a given state (*to exist*). Verbs usually are conjugated in a certain way to their speaker, though they aren't conjugated in every language. It will vary depending mostly upon which language exactly you're speaking. But a huge number of languages have this feature, called both verb inflection and verb conjugation. All that it means is that they are changed in a certain way to agree with any number of characteristics of either the subject or the object (generally the subject), such as gender, plurality, and perspective (first person, second person, third person). Languages which are based around this concept will generally require a lot of work to understand how verbs work and how you can make them come naturally. Languages which don't have this concept make up for the difficulty elsewhere. There are actually a lot more things to verbs, such as intransitive verbs vs. transitive verbs (which pertains to whether or not they utilize a direct object), linking verbs, and so on. It really depends upon the language that you're specifically studying as to how it implements it.

Objects - Objects are the things which are on the other side of the verb. This may sound obvious and vague, but the truth is that defining objects can be a little tricky. The general definition is usually something along the lines of "the word which is affected by the verb." This can be a little tricky, however. Objects are generally divided into two classes: direct objects and indirect objects. I make this distinction in every language book I write and am certain to make the lines between them very clear. There are a lot of ways to divide and define the two, but the way that I find most useful to describe the difference between the two is by making a very clear delineation between the required nature of the two. This is to say that if you have a direct object, you can't remove it from the sentence and have it makes sense, whereas indirect objects serve a purely contextual purpose. Consider the sentence "He writes the book with me." We can divide this into its parts: "He *mails* **the book** <u>with me</u>." In this case, the subject is left unstylized, the verb is italicized, the direct object is emboldened, and the indirect object is underlined. You can see easier now the relationship between the verb and the direct object. If you were to say "He mails with me.", it would make absolutely no sense at all. People would be wondering "he mails *what* with me?" The direct object is what answers that question of *what* in sentences. However, if we were to take out the indirect object instead, like so: "He mails the book", it would make perfect sense. Indirect objects most of the time do little more than provide context. The phrase "He says it to me." is similar: the *to me*, while essential to the point of the sentence, is purely contextual and the sentence would be grammatically sound without that.

    Anyhow, those are the three main components of a sentence across languages. It would serve you well to understand them all to the maximum capacity you can within your own language. Does the subject come before the verb? After? Where does the object go? Not every sentence in every language works like English sentences do. You have to remember that language has as much, if not more, societal deviation than separate cultures. The conditions which created any two given languages are never the same, and so they'll have grown differently and may have even had a completely different basis. For an example of this sort of growth, *PIE* was originally a subject object verb sentence, as were Ancient Greek and Latin. However, as they would grow and develop, they would change this order entirely. And it's not unusual for this sort of thing to happen over periods of vast linguistic growth. English, for example, dropped the idea of verb-second word order altogether.

    As you read through all of this, you should be simultaneously learning *how*. This is how you're going to build your foundation: learning exactly how all of it works. You aren't going to go very far if you don't take the time to do all of this.

    For subjects, it's imperative that you learn every possible subject pronoun and, a little later, every possible object pronoun. You're going to be using these and seeing these extensively for the simple reason that they're everywhere. There isn't a sentence which can work without a subject. Well, there are, but they aren't valid sentences generally. There are some sentences, such as Spanish, which allow you to drop the subject due to the conjugation, but this is for the simple reason that the subject is implied through the conjugation of the sentence. Conversely, French doesn't work in such a manner; you *have* to either say a subject pronoun or you have to mention a specific subject alongside a very specific article which denotes exactly what you're talking about. This is because all of the first-person verbs mesh together on their endings and you can only tell them apart if there's liaison involved, often. So regardless of what the specific system for subjects is within the language that you're going to be working with, it's your job to understand them to the best extent which you can.

    Now, speaking in terms of verbs, I've mentioned before my disdain for classroom style vocabulary learning, and going along with that, I don't think the best way to learn verbs is in that manner. However, and that's a big however, you do need to recognize verb inflection if there is such a thing, or any other manners of recognizing verbs so that you can actually work with and understand them, as well as recognize them when they show up in the text. Additionally, you really need to learn the basic verbs, and unfortunately, there will often be a lot of irregular verbs that are completely detached from any notion of normal conjugation or declension. Even in Chinese, which has *no* verb conjugation system, there are two verbs which have a marker afterwards that is irregular. These form naturally, honestly, after a long period of language speaking. This is exacerbated by the general lack of print or text reproduction technology for most of history. Alongside the general lack of literacy came a lack of standardization, which made it rather difficult to have any sort of uniformity among the language as it would grow and develop. So the changes which would occur were very massive and sweeping, and also led to some verbs losing any sort of standardized form. Perhaps such is a bit natural after several millennia of linguistic divergence, but I digress. You're going to have to practice 1) recognizing verb inflections for regular verbs, and recognizing those verbs when they pop up in the text and 2) at the *least*, the ten most common irregular verbs for the language that you're learning (if it should have that many; some don't.)

The only other trouble you'll run into in the sphere of verbs if you do those two things is understanding idiomatic expressions, or phrases which don't mean expressly what they say they mean. An example of an idiom in English would be "it's raining cats and dogs". It's not *literally* raining cats and dogs, but it is raining quite hard if one says such a thing. With that said, though, if you follow the language acquisition tips that I outline in the chapter after this one, you should these idioms through your personal translation efforts.

When it comes to verb tenses, you don't have to know every single tense. It's worthwhile for you to learn the most common past tense and future tense if they exist, though. For example, in French, this would be the passé composé and either the simple future or the *futur proche,* meaning "close future". I use French as an example because it's the language I know best, but this applies to any given language. Some languages don't have a "past tense" verb conjugation per se and have a different way of showing past tense. Either way, you're going to need to know how to use that part of speech, as well as understand how it will show up in both speech and text.

The last thing is the object. Objects generally aren't too terribly difficult to learn across languages and are typically actually one of the easier things of understand because most of the time, they'll be composed of either a noun, an article and a noun, or a preposition and a noun. The hard part is more understanding the articles and prepositions of the language so that you can recognize the indirect objects when you see them. Some languages do bizarre things with objects, but by studying the broad concept of objects within the language, then you'll be able to start to understand.

I just mentioned articles and prepositions. I do think it's absolutely necessary that you understand articles before you go any further with your language learning. This won't apply to every language - some languages don't have what we'd commonly refer to as articles, or they have them in a far different way than we'd recognize. However, it's still worth researching and finding your answer so that you can learn as to whether the given language does have them or not. Articles are things which specify the *number* and *location* of a given noun. For example, if I were to say "I ate *a* slice of pizza", it would indicate that that I ate some non-specific piece of pizza. This is commonly referred to as an indefinite article. If I were to say "I ate *the* slice of pizza", it's implied that I'm referring to a very explicit slice of pizza, not just any slice off of the street. Maybe somebody asked me what happened to a very specific slice of pizza, and I responded in accordance. This is called a *definite* article. There are also other types of articles. "This" and "that" could be considered articles - "I ate *this* slice of pizza" refers to a specific slice which you are demonstrating, where "I ate *that* slice of pizza" means you're referring to a specific slice which is elsewhere from you. The simple correlation for this is usually "this" -> "here", "that" -> "there". Articles are essential because, especially with languages like Danish and Swedish, if you don't know them, they will almost certainly get lost in the text. It's not that they're hard to understand, but it's that if you *don't* understand them, you're at a massive disadvantage.

On a related note to articles and prepositions, you may run across the notion of "gendered" nouns. This doesn't refer to a physical characteristic so much as a linguistic development. Nouns, especially in Romance languages, which have genders have such because it produces vowel harmony, and they just happen to sound best with the articles and pronouns which would be used to reference male and female human beings. Some languages will also have a *neuter* gender which will make it an even more confusing mess. But really, it doesn't quite matter on the origin of these, what matters more is that you learn the nuances of noun gender for your particular language if such a thing exists for it.

Anyhow, the next thing that you're going to want to learn is prepositions. It's important to learn at least the most basic of prepositions, because prepositions are what allow you to express yourself on a higher level. Prepositions open the door for not only idiom but for phrases which allow you to imply or explicitly state an object's location. Prepositions in English were always explained to me in grade school as "places where a squirrel can go": a squirrel can go in, out, around, through, and so forth... it wasn't a perfect explanation and it certainly is lacking in the proper nuance, but it does fit the bill pretty well. Some prepositions are absolutely essential, such as *à* in French: it's used for both location as well as a helping article in transitive verbs and general things of that nature. You have to seriously take time to learn at least the most basic of prepositions in whatever language that you're trying to learn so that you can better know what you're working with as you go forward.

What's more is that you need to learn basic conversational phrases. This is because these vary from language to language and it can be a little bizarre trying to translate some of them directly because a lot of them have no direct translation. Some of them have been the same for centuries while other aspects of the language have changed, which can make it a really bizarre experience. So the best thing to do, really, is to learn them as their own unit. Learn things like "hello", "goodbye", "thank you", and "please", alongside how to get to a certain place and how to ask for help. The other plus side is that since you've already looked a great deal into the formation of verbs and subjects and objects, you'll be able to pick each out of the sentence and likely increase your vocabulary to a certain extent.

    The last thing that you really need to focus on picking up in terms of background knowledge is learning how to ask *questions* in the given language. This, too, will vary from language to language, and rather greatly at that. But asking questions is a major part of any conducive conversation. On top of that, you're going to have to work with questions in order to ask people how to get around or for the help that you'll inevitably need.

    After you've built a solid foundation and you feel like you know the most essential parts of the language well, even if your vocabulary isn't excellent, then you're ready to move forward into the immersive part of this method.

You are halfway done!

Congratulations on making it to the halfway point of the journey. Many try and give up long before even getting to this point, so you are to be congratulated on this. You have shown that you are serious about getting better every day. I am also serious about improving my life, and helping others get better along the way. To do this I need your feedback. Click on the link below and take a moment to let me know how this book has helped you. If you feel there is something missing or something you would like to see differently, I would love to know about it. I want to ensure that as you and I improve, this book continues to improve as well. Thank you for taking the time to ensure that we are all getting the most from each other.

Chapter 3: Immerse Yourself

A few years ago, I tried to learn Latin from a book. It was a rather archaic book written by a well-meaning professor sometime in the 1970s or 1980s; well, I say that, but the reality is that it was written a bit later, likely in the mid-1990s, its methodology just *seemed* so outdated. This is when I began to realize a lot of the structural problems of language learning and why people become so disenfranchised with it so fast.

We already talked in chapter one about how people tend to give up learning a language because it's just "simply not for them." When they say this, I sigh, and not for them and not out of pity, but rather out of regret that we've managed to build a manner of educating people on languages that manages not to *teach* a many people who fall into these language learning classes, but rather to have them *pass a test*.

It's my firm belief, as I've already said, that not only are people *able* to learn, but they're *made* to learn language. However, just as we tend to take the fun out of a great many things in academia, language learning itself has been relegated to being a book-y study-wrought subject rather than what it actually is: an opportunity to meet new souls that you've never met before, to talk to and intertwine with people that you normally never would have because you don't even speak the same language.

See, language learning is actually a beautiful experience. By learning a language, you're allowing yourself to see into a whole new world of culture and alternative thought. Some places are a bigger departure from your customs than others, but every single place has its own unique story. What's neat is that language not only allows you to *experience* this story, but you also get to *get* some of this story from the language itself. My favorite example of this is Spanish. Spanish is a language of a territory in heavy dispute and intrinsic conflict for centuries. In their language, you find the culture of a great numerous conquests against the Spanish, most notably by the Arabs who had taken control of Spain for some 3 or 4 centuries in the first and second millennium. This is evident in the fact that Spanish had actually adopted a huge number of words from those who had conquered them - Arabic words which would come to represent either new concepts in Spain or replace the go-to word for old concepts. Of course, these weren't entirely pervasive, but their presence is noteworthy nonetheless. If you were to open a Spanish dictionary and flip back to the opening pages, you'd see several pages of words which begin with "al", which means they were more than likely taken from Arabic, which had an article "*al*" meaning "*the*".

So how we manage to turn that into a dull classroom experience is *beyond* me. Language learning itself is little more than a door to a whole new world of experiences. Sure, the lock may be a bit difficult to figure out, exactly, but the contents on the other side of the door make it worth it.

That's beside the point, though: language is an *intrinsically social* concept. It would make absolutely zero sense if you learned a new language to talk about something that you don't care about. So why would you try to go forward with learning a language if it meant doing so in a manner which you don't care about and frankly couldn't really care *less* about? It's an absolute recipe for disaster.

What I propose to you instead is a method I've developed during my language studies which I refer to as *usage-based vocabulary learning*. There's actually another method and component to this whole lesson: *passion-based immersion*.

Let me break this down.

The idea behind this theory is rather simple: we learn best when we're actually using things that we learn. Likewise, for the vast majority of people who would be categorized as kinetic learners, they learn by active usage and reinforcement of concepts and scouring out solutions if they can't find them in the first place.

What I've developed is a far more hands-on method to vocabulary increasing than what the norm is. Note that I'm not completely disowning the concept of traditional vocabulary learning, and it can, in fact, be beneficial. Rather, what I'm decrying is the idea of using *solely* traditional vocabulary learning and taking in heaps of words and then never using them again until a long time down the road.

My train of thought in developing this was actually based off of an experience I had a while back when I was learning French, my first secondary language. I had been trodding along for a while but hardly making genuine progress. I had taken it all throughout high school and would occasionally dabble with it but didn't make a lot of sense of it. It sounds really small, but at one point I discovered that the United Kingdom equivalent to the United States word "eggplant" was "aubergine", which reminded me of the French term I'd remembered some years ago but long forgotten, or at least certainly wouldn't have been able to recall. I suppose the association between the English and the French term jarred my recollection. But at that point, I started thinking about how I remembered that word solely by making a connection, and I realized that past a certain point, the totality of language learning is the gentle art of making things click.

It seems like a rather small incident and it was, for certain - but the consequences of it, the train of thought which resulted, made me get back to learning French by way of *practicing* it. If I ever needed a word, the beauty of the information age meant that I could just go to a website and find a nearly direct translation, along with a sentence and comparative context. That was a huge boon to my ability to speak French well and I realized that I was growing quickly and had made on my own a realization that every great language learner has made: language learning, whether it be your first language or your fifth language, always occurs because you see/hear a word you don't know, analyze the context, and give that word a context. So if it works that way, I reasoned, why couldn't the opposite be true? Why couldn't we have a *context* that we didn't know how to explain, and learn the language through adjustment and effort to those given contexts? The same mechanism of making things "click" is present within both actions, so long as you know the basics of the language that the words you're presenting for your context aren't either outlandishly difficult or impossible to parse given your understanding of a language.

Anyway, having made this realization and being the aspiring poet that I was at that point, I took to writing quite a bit of poetry. This helped me greatly in learning the uses of various words I *did* know as I would research them for correctness, as well as allowing me to practice them, and it also helped me to increase my vocabulary because I had specific ideas that I was trying to convey.

That's why one of the pillars which I recommend to you as a language learner is the following: find a way to **use** your language. There is absolutely no way around this step. As a new speaker, you may feel a tad uncomfortable using it around other people, and that's okay (even though you'll have to sometime.) What I recommend that you do instead is start writing a nightly journal, recounting your day in the language which you were trying to learn, and expressing any thoughts you might have otherwise in the language as well. Do this daily, regardless of whether you're talking to people in the given language yet or not. There is no way around this task. It's simple, it doesn't take terribly long, and it's the most effective form of study that you can undertake: that which allows you to truly *express*.

There are a great number of reasons that you should take my advice and write a nightly journal in the language of your choosing. The first, of course, is that it allows you to practice the language. The second is that you're going to naturally pick up a lot more words. You'll get a lot of experience using common expressions and you'll find yourself feeling like more of a natural when it comes to things like irregular verbs or noun declension. Even things like verb conjugation will come out to be much easier for you. Write your *thoughts*, studiously, and if you ever have a question about whether a certain verb tense exists in the language you're studying, or whether a certain word exists, then I implore you to *research it*.

The truth is that you have *got* to learn vocabulary somehow. There are a lot of ways to do it. But when it comes between a method which works on our intuitive capacity to learn and utilize language, and one which just requires rote memorization of given concepts which we may or may not use at a later point, I will always opt for the first.

This is the first time that I've published this method, so my sample size is rather small; in fact, it consists solely of myself. But I genuinely believe that this specific method of acquiring new vocabulary in a language is far better than the traditional method.

As I said though, there's still a lot of room for traditional vocabulary learning in the sense of non-usage memorization techniques. In fact, as a standalone tactic, there's nothing intrinsically *wrong* with them as a primary language learning route. It's just that there's an option which is *better* as a primary language learning route, because it actively engages you. I genuinely believe that to some degree we've surpassed the archaic notions of rote memorization, because when I hear that I can't help recalling about the tutored children in Greece who were required to recite epic poems.

With that said, there is certainly and without a doubt a place for them as a *secondary* method of language acquisition, and I do certainly encourage you to use them in this manner. I believe that the most well-known example of these rote-memorization services being used as a sort of way to reinforce grammar and explore vocabulary is the *Duolingo* service available at (http://duolingo.com), though if you're learning Chinese you may be inclined to look at "Hello Chinese" (http://hellochinese.cc) which is very similar to China.

I think that grammar and vocabulary are two distinct phenomena, in a way. I think that grammar requires independent case-related study - you aren't going to remember how to form, for example, the imperfect tense in Italian if you aren't actively using it in any way - so you should research it as you need it in your personal writings and so that you're prepared to use it *next* time you need to. Basically everything about this language acquisition method is diametrically opposed to anything that requires you to memorize something *before* you run across it naturally.

In other words, I don't feel like there's anything very organic about learning a language by remembering words on a page. And likewise, I think that since it's such an inorganic method of language acquisition, I don't think that people who decide to use this specific route of language acquisition are going to go terribly far at all with it.

I know what you're thinking: "If I wait to learn these things until I need them, then how am I going to know how to use them when I need them?"

I understand that concern entirely. I will say that your basic introductions to a language should always include how to form the past tense or, in the few languages for which there isn't a specific past tense, how to indicate something happened in the past, just in case you run into a need for it. However, here are two facts:

1) When I say you need to learn things as you encounter a need to learn them, I don't mean that every time you need a word should be when you're out in the streets needing help for this or that. What I mean is that you

need to practice a direct yet detached method of language acquisition which focuses on the *organic* process of interpreting and understanding new terms as opposed to the process which focuses entirely on the sole acquisition of new terms that many language learning courses devolve into.
2) Kindness is a human trait. No matter how much people tell you otherwise, for the vast majority of people, the default will always be kindness. So if you walk into a place in a foreign country and have to fumble with the language, they won't be angry and they won't be upset with you. Learning somebody else's language is a show of *respect*, not disrespect, and they will only respect you and try to help you for learning their culture. Most people are proud of where they come from to some extent or another, and anything respect paid to the culture of where they call "home" is looked kindly upon. So there's nothing wrong with speaking a Pidgin version of a language or hardly knowing how to conjugate verbs (though this isn't realistic if you're working with the language on a nightly basis).

The reason I say all of this is to articulate why I don't think that programs like Duolingo are great if they're the *only* source that you're working with. I just feel as though they fail in an essential way. If you are working with two concepts which beg development on their own accord, then the experience of learning both is diluted.

So I'm sure at this point you're skeptical. This is a little bit of a bizarre way to learn a language, I understand. But try it and you'll understand.

Let me now move onto the other part, which will hopefully clear up any residual concerns you have about the language learning process I'm suggesting, and the reason this chapter is called "Immerse yourself".

There are two sides to immersion: *ingoing* and *outgoing*. *Outgoing* is what we just talked about: the actual private usage of the language in order to develop your ability to speak in it. This is one essential part of this paradigm of language acquisition.

The other part then is obviously *incoming immersion*. These are the influences in the language that you're taking in from the *outside*. Language learning ideally should include a beneficial balance of both of these. I frankly have yet to figure out exactly what this balance should be, though.

So what, in my eyes, makes up *incoming immersion*? Anything that you experience in the language that allows you to make sense of something. These are things which act on those "make it click" mechanisms in our brains in order to connect certain lines between words and meaning in the new language. There are a lot of ways that you can actually achieve this.

The first is rather obvious: change the language of your phone and computer to the language you're wishing to learn. This specific suggestion may work better for languages in the Indo-European language family as it's much easier to "extrapolate" the meanings of vague phrases when they have a similar formation. This is pertinent when it comes to technology because certain things *are* in longer, complete sentences, but a huge number of things are not, like application names or menus in the Windows file explorer such as "This Computer". This isn't exclusively true, however, and if you have a knowledge of how the language is written, pronounced, and structured, it's probably in your best interest to immerse yourself in that manner.

The second is obvious as well: use subtitles to your advantage. Netflix has thousands of titles streaming that are available in multiple languages, as well as a huge number of films which are available in both English and alternative language subtitles as well. This can be extremely conducive to those "make it click" mechanisms because you're actively enthralled by the thing that you're watching.

My recommendation, should you decide to go along with this, is to start with English audio and subtitles in your given language *first*. After you're comfortable with the language, I would then switch over to the audio in your given language and English subtitles. The reason for this is that it's really easy to be confused or thrown off by a language's accent at first as a language learner, and I don't think that it's ultimately very conducive to try to wean words apart in the native language and give them an English meaning from the English subtitles if you don't know very much about the language. That sort of thing is more for learning supplementary words and idioms once you have a firm enough grasp of the language in other contexts. As you're starting out, you 110% should start with English audio, just because it allows you to get used to reading the given language and acquainting the many words you don't know at that point to their English equivalent rather than the converse. The power of audio only goes so far, and in English, you already know where words start and end. As a beginner in a new language, you often don't have such a privilege.

So as we go forward with the idea of ingoing immersion, we're coming to the topic that I mentioned earlier and that I think is ultimately one of the two most important things to take away from this chapter: *passion-based immersion*.

So what do I mean by this? It probably sounds a tad pretentious, I'm aware, but the meaning is pure.

Human interests arise as forces in society as people group together in order to talk about them and join in solidarity over their admiration for the given topic. That is to say that often these topics will cross the general lines of linguistic division and carry over across languages.

What's more is that we always learn better when it's something that we care about, or connected in a way, even only tangentially, to something that we care about. We're more likely to forge mental connections and remember things which need to be remembered if they're connected to something that we ultimately care about rather than something that we, well, don't.

This theory builds upon that idea. The premise is simple: take the things you like and take advantage of that in order to learn a new language. But the manifestation can be a tad difficult.

The exact advice for carrying this out really depends ultimately upon what your passions even *are*. Regardless of what they are, the chances are much better than the converse that the region where the language you're learning is either spoken currently or has had a presence before will have *some* sort of connection to the topic.

For example, let's take World War II. A lot of people are *greatly* interested in World War II as a general topic. By learning French or Russian, you could read about the events from either a French or a Soviet perspective respectively.

I guess the point I'm trying to make in this instance is that earlier, I mentioned that learning a language opens the door to a lot of culture. Well, by this point I've already enumerated many times over how important being passionate is to the idea of language learning and how much it will help you.

So what I'm telling you to do here is to connect those two ideals of regional culture and passion in some manner so that you can find a book written in the source language that you'll actually *want* to read. Every night, translate either a page or a paragraph depending upon both how big the book is and how much time you have to dedicate to this. At first, you're going to be fumbling around a lot and encountering a lot of words you don't know - that's absolutely fine and frankly it's to be very expected. However, you should after a while make your way to the end of the book, at which point you can get another book related to your passions and repeat the process.

There are a lot of resources for translation, but I absolutely can't get enough of WordReference (http://wordreference.com). They have extensive dictionaries for a great number of languages and, on top of that, they have a wonderful system for searching up not only words but also idioms, expressions, and common phrases.

After a while, you should make your way through the book and reread it. Translate again any words that you don't understand entirely, but this time around they should be much fewer.

This will inevitably be time-consuming, but learning a language works on an inverse relationship of *effort* and *time*: the more *effort* and study that you expend towards learning a language, the less overall *time* it will take you to learn a language. So what benefits does this serve, exactly? Many!

- This method allows you to work with something that you care about. As I've already said, this makes you much more likely to internalize the information than doing it in an alternative manner.
- Working with a new language constantly will allow you to become much stronger with it.
- There's a fixed motive of finish a page/paragraph which makes it easier to go through with, but not quite laborious since you care about the topic at hand.

I think the biggest thing which makes it a great asset is the fact that you *are* mentally connected to the topic after all, though. That means that it's going to be much easier for you to absorb the words that you translate.

I don't think you need to drill yourself learning vocabulary as you're starting out, though. I think you need to focus more on patterns. Every language has patterns. For example, adverbs in English end in -*ly*; in Spanish, they end in -*mente*; in French, they end in -*ment*, and so on. So many people become disenfranchised with learning languages because it just becomes a game of constant memorization. They'll be so disheartened and stressed out by having to memorize *x* set of words, and that stress actually makes it far harder to learn.

This is where I should give yet another disclaimer: I don't think that flashcard learning methods are explicitly bad, or any other popular method of vocabulary learning. I think it can be useful if you take the right mindset about it. However, once more, I don't think it should be your primary learning vehicle. Your primary learning vehicle should be *personal experience*, no questions asked. There's nothing that will benefit you so much as immersing yourself in something that you care about.

Chapter 4: Usage

So, we're nearing the end of the book and one thing has become incredibly apparent: none of this work that you've done matters if you aren't going to find a way to use the language and reinforce the things which you've already learned.

I mean sure, reading and writing will get you to a certain extent, but what really helps a person understand a language is, frankly, *using* it. Not in journals, not in just watching the television with subtitles or dubbed audio, but with actually using the language that you've developed it.

Thanks to the things we worked on in the first chapter, I dearly hope that you're at a point where you feel confident with not only what you do know but what you *don't* know, as well as with your ability to transfer both to the real world.

The simple fact is that as you speak to other people, you are going to make mistakes, and you are going to make quite a few. But it's really not so bad; we make mistakes in our *native* language all the time, yet nobody is embarrassed about them. Think about all the people who get extremely confused on the usage differences of "your" and "you're", or of "to" and "too" and "two". People tend not to notice these -- in fact, they proclaim them proudly by virtue of not noticing them.

But the thing is that you've got to do whatever you can to get out of your comfort zone and start speaking another language. You have to actually *use* the language. Strike up conversations with new people who speak the language. If you are studying at home, not abroad, then it may benefit you to find a pen-pal or a Skype partner. There are lots of these in lots of places, I recommend http://language-exchanges.org in order to find people that you can converse in your new language on Skype with. However, you can also go to http://italki.com, which is a paid service but very popular thanks to certain personalities promoting it.

Another thing that you can do is head to http://meetup.com. This is a beautiful resource for meeting other people who practice the same language that you do, and generally has people who are at multiple skill levels, from beginner to intermediate to expert to fluent. All that you do is go to the site and type in your location and type in the language as the keyword. Then search. I was able to find local groups with ease. If you live anywhere near a city, as most people do, you should be able to find some group which is somewhat relevant to your interests.

The purpose in all of these things I'm suggesting is to give you the chance to practice talking under pressure, as well as to meet new people. When you meet new people who speak a different language, you can subconsciously forge a barrier with them. It's somewhat like a mask at a masquerade; you can see behind it, but why would you want to? When you meet someone under the pretense of speaking another language, you speak to them *in that language*. You can work off of each other to develop if you're at about the same level and if they're at a better level (I advise making friends with at least one person who is at a better level linguistically than you are) then you can very easily be corrected instantaneously and try to have genuine conversations with real people.

The thing too is that when you meet people in this manner, you're still meeting *people*. People with childhoods, stories, alma maters and degrees, pets and children, girlfriends and boyfriends, people who have traveled, people who were raised in a different culture, and so on and so forth. The chances are very great that if you meet a person through this method, you're going to actually *want* to talk to them in the language, which will even further drive your desire to learn the language and speak it very well.

This is one of the shortest chapters in the book, I know, but its importance can't be understated. You're doing yourself a major disservice if you opt to not try to meet others who speak the language. It's only through positive real life reinforcement that you're going to develop into a master of whatever language it is that you've decided to practice.

Conclusion

Thank for making it through to the end of *Learn Languages: The fastest and easiest way to learn any foreign language,* let's hope it was informative and able to provide you with all of the tools you need to achieve your goals whatever it may be.

The next step is to take these things we've talked about and apply them. I've made it more than abundantly clear just how you can do that. You need to be the one to go outside of your comfort zone. Use words you don't quite understand, conjugate verbs in conversation that you're not quite familiar with, do anything and everything. It is only through use and reinforcement that you'll learn a language in a short amount of time.

I genuinely hope that the help I've tried to provide throughout the course of this book is something that you've found useful. It's my sincere goal as somebody who cares very genuinely about linguistics that you may use these tips in order to become a better speaker of another language, and that you may also be exposed to the concepts which I care so dearly about.

Finally, if you found this book useful in any way, a review on Amazon is always appreciated!

Help me improve this book

While I have never met you, if you made it through this book I know that you are the kind of person that is wanting to get better and is willing to take on tough feedback to get to that point. You and I are cut from the same cloth in that respect. I am always looking to get better and I wish to not just improve myself, but also this book. If you have positive feedback, please take the time to leave a review. It will help other find this book and it can help change a life in the same way that it changed yours. If you have constructive feedback, please also leave a review. It will help me better understand what you, the reader, need to make significant improvements in your life. I will take your feedback and use it to improve this book so that it can become more powerful and beneficial to all those who encounter it.

Free membership into the Mastermind Self

Development Group!

For a limited time, you can join the Mastermind Self Development Group for free! You will receive videos and articles from top authorities in self development as well as a special group only offers on new books and training programs. There will also be a monthly member only draw that gives you a chance to win any book from your Kindle wish list!

If you sign up through this link http://www.mastermindselfdevelopment.com/specialreport you will also get a special free report on the Wheel of Life. This report will give you a visual look at your current life and then take you through a series of exercises that will help you plan what your perfect life looks like. The workbook does not end there; we then take you through a process to help you plan how to achieve that perfect life. The process is very powerful and has the potential to change your life forever. Join the group now and start to change your life!
http://www.mastermindselfdevelopment.com/specialreport

You will also love these other great titles from Mastermind Self Development!

You will want to check out these other great titles Mastermind Self Development. All available in the Kindle store or you can just click on covers below.

http://viewbook.at/selflove

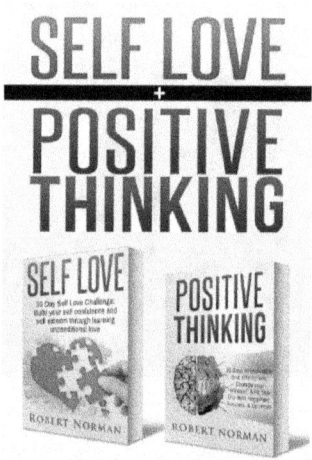

http://mybook.to/positivelove

Learn French

A Fast and Easy Guide for Beginners to Learn Conversational French

Free membership into the Mastermind Self Development Group!

For a limited time, you can join the Mastermind Self Development Group for free! You will receive videos and articles from top authorities in self development as well as a special group only offers on new books and training programs. There will also be a monthly member only draw that gives you a chance to win any book from your Kindle wish list!

If you sign up through this link http://www.mastermindselfdevelopment.com/specialreport you will also get a special free report on the Wheel of Life. This report will give you a visual look at your current life and then take you through a series of exercises that will help you plan what your perfect life looks like. The workbook does not end there; we then take you through a process to help you plan how to achieve that perfect life. The process is very powerful and has the potential to change your life forever. Join the group now and start to change your life!
http://www.mastermindselfdevelopment.com/specialreport

Table of Contents

Introduction

Chapter 1: French - how does it work?

Chapter 2: Pronunciation

Chapter 3: Past and Future Tenses

Chapter 4: Questions and Objects

Chapter 5: Adjectives, Adverbs, Conjunctions, and Prepositions

Chapter 6: Conversational Necessities

Conclusion

© Copyright 2016 by Mastermind Self Development All rights reserved.

The follow eBook is reproduced below with the goal of providing information that is as accurate and reliable as possible. Regardless, purchasing this eBook can be seen as consent to the fact that both the publisher and the author of this book are in no way experts on the topics discussed within and that any recommendations or suggestions that are made herein are for entertainment purposes only. Professionals should be consulted as needed prior to undertaking any of the action endorsed herein.

This declaration is deemed fair and valid by both the American Bar Association and the Committee of Publishers Association and is legally binding throughout the United States.

Furthermore, the transmission, duplication or reproduction of any of the following work including specific information will be considered an illegal act irrespective of if it is done electronically or in print. This extends to creating a secondary or tertiary copy of the work or a recorded copy and is only allowed with express written consent from the Publisher. All additional right reserved.

The information in the following pages is broadly considered to be a truthful and accurate account of facts and as such any inattention, use or misuse of the information in question by the reader will render any resulting actions solely under their purview. There are no scenarios in which the publisher or the original author of this work can be in any fashion deemed liable for any hardship or damages that may befall them after undertaking information described herein.

Additionally, the information in the following pages is intended only for informational purposes and should thus be thought of as universal. As befitting its nature, it is presented without assurance regarding its prolonged validity or interim quality. Trademarks that are mentioned are done without written consent and can in no way be considered an endorsement from the trademark holder.

Introduction

Congratulations on downloading **Learn French** and thank you for doing so.

The following chapters will discuss what is in my opinion the best and most efficient way to learn the French language.

If you're reading this, it's of course because you have an interest in learning French. There are many reasons that you may have such an interest. Maybe you've gotten a job offer which would require you to relocate to Québec or France or Morocco. Maybe you're having a hard time keeping up with your college or high school French classes and looking for some extracurricular guidance. Maybe it's just for the pure purpose of leisure and you don't really have any additional motives.

Regardless of what your goal ultimately is, my goal is to help you meet it. Throughout the course of this book, you're going to be learning quite a lot of things regarding French. In the first chapter, we'll be covering the bare essentials of sentence structure and verbiage, as well as covering essential differences between French and English. In the second, we're going to be talking more about the precise pronunciation rules of French. In the third, we're going to be talking about the past and future tenses. The fourth is going to be talking more about direct and indirect object pronouns. The fifth chapter is going to discuss higher end grammatical concepts. The fifth chapter is going to discuss basic French conversation and give you some useful phrases for travel.

There are plenty of books on this subject on the market, thanks again for choosing this one! Every effort was made to ensure it is full of as much useful information as possible, please enjoy!

Chapter 1: French - how does it work?

So many people all the time everywhere make an extreme error in learning languages: they fail to look at it in the context óf a *language* and instead try to turn it into a game of memorization. This doesn't work. There are good and bad ways to learn language, and if at the end of the day, all you have to show for yourself are a few phrases memorized off of some flash cards, then frankly, you're learning the language in a bad way.

I've been trying to communicate how to learn languages for a very long time and I'm still having a hard time determining whether I think language learning is an art or a science. Regardless, the truth is that there is no one perfect way to learn a language, because we all learn in terribly different ways, which makes it nigh impossible to pin down one singular way which would most work.

However, there are certain natural mechanisms for picking up languages that people of average intelligence and greater can utilize in order to pick up language really easily.

We don't come out of the womb learning a language. We come out as a blank slate. We have the *ability* to speak language, but it's unformed; a baby born in China will learn a form of Chinese, and a baby born in England will learn English.

Babies can't read flash cards. And while our natural propensity to learn a language demonstrably goes down as a person ages, there are numerous reasons for this which aren't normally accounted for.

A child has to learn a language in order to survive and communicate, and has an easy time learning a language due to the fact that it's completely immersed in it.

There are language learning gurus out there who are polyglots because they put themselves in similar situations in order to learn language: the immerse themselves near entirely in the language by traveling from place to place and making it so that they have to speak and understand the language to survive and communicate.

Now, it's likely not feasible for you to up and relocate to Quebec or France just in order to learn a language. But that's not to say that we can't trigger the same sort of intuitive language learning processes that these language learning gurus and these children are tapping into.

In other words, this entire method is based around the idea that if you have the proper springboard and the proper background, you can do any number of things with the language that you wish simply by natural self guided immersion and active effort in learning the language.

My goal in this book isn't to give you a vocabulary list to memorize, nor is it to give you a precise grammatical explanation of every single thing (though I'll certainly try to give accurate and succinct explanations), but rather it's to help you streamline the natural language learning processes so that you don't, well, forget every last thing that you learn in the process of reading this book.

The way that they taught you to learn languages in high school was wrong. Cut and dry, 100%, it was not the right way to go about it. Well, it was and it wasn't. It was right in some capacities - you likely had to listen to and repeat phrases in the class, which was solid basic immersion. But the idea of regurgitating vocab words onto a test is bizarre and ludicrous and just a way to ensure that you forget the very words you learned the following year.

The only way to avoid this sort of situation is by actively using the vocabulary and words that you've learned, but the reality is that a lot of high schools - especially ones with less funding - don't try particularly hard with their pen pal projects or anything of that nature.

Anyhow, the purpose of this book is to *streamline* the process of learning a language intuitively. There are a few different ways in which I'm going to try earnestly to do this. The first is by explaining the *differences* between English and French.

You may be wondering, "why would you do that? Why not start with the similarities?"

Well, the simple answer is because any language has more happening in common with another language than it has happening differently. This may sound bizarre, but think about it - every language is just a form of communication. There are various differences between them but ultimately they're all attempting to accomplish the same essential key concept: the usage of verbal cues in order to denote or tell a given thing.

However, for all the similarities, languages can also be incredibly *different*. For example, if I were going to try to tell the similarities between English and Japanese, the list would be incredibly short, by mere virtue of the fact that English and Japanese have little truly in common. Grammatically, they are incredibly different beasts. On top of this, the vocabulary is very different. It's much easier to make you understand the ways in which Japanese and English *are* different than try to expect you to latch onto the things that are.

When you're told things that are similar between languages, you latch onto those concepts. You're unaware of the vast amount of differences and you may, in fact, make very simple mistakes. One common such mistake in French is the combination of the existence and state verb *être* with the present participle of another verb.

In English, we use this to construct the present continuous tense. For example:

I *am eating*.

He *is playing*.

They *are walking*.

However, this isn't such the case in French. The equivalent phrases would be along the lines of:

Je *suis mangant*.

Il *est jouant*.

Ils *sont marchant*.

But this isn't correct at all, and in fact sound particularly bizarre and out of place to other French speakers. The correct way would be to conjugate the infinitive of the directly referenced verb (to eat, to play, to walk) for the present indicative and completely leave the *être* (to be) verb out of it:

Je *mange*.

Il *joue*.

Ils *marchent*.

There are a great number of differences between English and French as such that you'll somewhat naturally pick up as we go along, but that I'll point out regardless.

We'll be getting a lot more into the exact pronunciation of the given sounds in French in the next chapter, but for right now, I just want to give you some phrases and verbs that you can work with *as we speak*. Throughout this book, I'm going to be giving you pronunciation guides where possible. Some sounds are hard to approximate without using a phonetic alphabet, however.

One particular sound is the sound made in "je" and "le" and similar words. You may be tempted, especially if you have experience in other Romance languages where the sounds are very cut and dry, to pronounce these as "jeh" and "leh", as in "JEffrey" or "LEt's go", but you can't do that. This sound is actually much closer to the *oo* sound in *book* (U.S. English).

For phonetic purposes, this specific sound will be represented with the letters *uu*.

It's also important to bear in mind going forward that every *r* in Modern French is pronounced in a very guttural trill, quite similar to the German *r*, though not quite as intense. (though it's particularly hard for a language to be anywhere near as intense as German is, truthfully.) The only exception is generally in rural communities in Quebec or among the elderly in Southern France. Otherwise, the sound is guttural and produced from airflow at the back of the throat. It can be difficult to ascertain at first, but you can find YouTube videos concerning the French *r* to help you to understand it.

So if I were to write the following phrase:

Je prends un sandwich. *(I'll take/have a sandwich.)*

I would write the pronunciation for it as such:

juu PRAHND uh(n) sand-WEECH

The *n* in parentheses denotes that the consonant should be barely uttered and heard. This is a scale which takes practice, and plays into a major part of French pronunciation, as we'll cover in the next chapter. For now, just follow my pronunciation text, because French pronunciation is an independent fish to fry that I don't want to tackle in this chapter.

There are still more differences between French and English, and it's really important to bear these in mind as you go forward, too.

First off, they are not pronounced similarly, at all. There will be several cognates that you'll run into that look quite similar to the English phrase but are pronounced nothing the same. Take, for example, the word "horrible". In French, the *h* is silent, the *r* would be guttural, and the *ble* consonant, which would sound like "bull" in English, sounds like "bluu" in French. So we go from *HOR-ih-bull* to *or-EEH-bluu*. *Il y a un grand différence entre les deux!* (There's a big difference between the two!)

That's not even including *false cognates* which you need to be incredibly wary of. Take for instance the word *terrible*. It also exists in French, where in a literary sense, it means something very similar to the English "terrible". However, if you were to ask a French person how they're doing, and they said "*pas terrible*", you may think they're saying "not bad" or "not terrible", but this isn't the case. In fact, *terrible* (tuu-REEH-bluu) in the colloquial sense means "great". So "*pas terrible*" really means "not great" or "not the best".

Going beyond that, a lot of things are somewhat topsy turvy in French. Take the phrase "*yaourt aux fruits*". This means "yogurt with fruit". However, "*aux*" is a contraction of "*à les*", meaning "to the" or "at the". The typical French word for "with" would indeed be "*avec*", as in "*Je vais aller au MGC avec mes copains*" ("I'm going to the mall with my friends."). However, "with" doesn't have as many uses in French as it does in English, and to express the innate quality of something, or the idea of something belonging to something else in a categorical sense, you use à rather than avec.

One last super important difference that we're going to cover at this given moment is saying your occupation. In English, we say "I am *a professor*" or "I am *a butcher*". However, the French leave this article out. To them, an occupation is an intrinsic quality, which somewhat makes sense if you think about it. So instead of saying "*Je suis un professeur*" (I am a professor), the French would rather say

"*Je suis professeur*" (literally 'I am professor').

Basic sentence structure

Anyhow, let's get to the meat of this chapter, because there's still quite a bit left to cover: subjects and verbs. This is the basis of every single sentence we speak. I'm sure that, by now, you know what a subject is. A *subject* is the word which denotes the performer of an action.

My dog **is** big.

In this sentence, *my dog* is the subject, where **is** is the verb (to be). Every language has a specific order in which they put subjects, objects, and verbs (an object being the *direct recipient* of an action, such as "*I* **love** cats", where "cats" is the object).

Subject pronouns

In English, we use sentence pronouns quite often. In fact, we use them in nearly every sentence!

Just to prove it, I'm going to type those two sentences again and underline the subject pronouns.

In English, we use sentence pronouns quite often. In fact, we use them in nearly every sentence!

So what is a sentence pronoun? A sentence pronoun is anything which replaces giving the direct name of something in the sentence. Take for example the sentence "John plays basketball."

Normally, if we've already brought John up as the topic of conversation, we can contextually replace his name and still have it be clear that we're talking about him specifically. We would do this by saying "he plays basketball."

Then, we use *we, I,* and *you* per standard, because there's not really a first or second direct *noun*. All direct nouns are by their nature in the third person. If your name were Janet, and you were asking me for directions, I wouldn't say "Janet needs to go to the light and turn left." The *you* would imply that I'm speaking *directly* to you, and the fact that I'm talking to you directly conversely implies that I need to use *you* in the first place, because the fact that I'm talking directly *to* someone and not directly *of* someone puts the sentence in the second person. Thus, I would say "You need to go to the light and turn left."

In English, we have several different subject pronouns. However, we still have less than French, miraculously.

Here are the ones that we mainly use in English:

I - first person singular.

you	-	second person singular.
He, she, it	-	third person singular
we	-	first person plural
they	-	third person plural

French, likewise, has numerous. They also have something we don't: a second person plural. We do have them, but they're informal and unstandardized. For example, in the Southern U.S. you may hear "y'all", and up north and in Britain you'll often hear "you guys". However, we don't have a singular word to refer to multiple people, and they do.

They also have the concept of *formality*. This means that in the second person singular formation, they will use different words depending entirely upon who they're talking to. For example, if you're talking to somebody you just met, someone older than you, or someone in a position of authority over you, you will always use the formal second-person pronoun, which coincidentally is also the second person plural. You use the informal second-person form, the equivalent of English "you" and German "du", when you're around people younger than you, family members, or people that you have met more than once.

The French pronouns are as follows:

Je (juu)	-	first person singular
Tu (too)	-	second person singular
Il/elle (il/el)	-	third person singular
Nous (noo)	-	first person plural
Vous (voo) formal	-	second person plural / first person singular
Ils/elles (il/el) *elles* for females	-	third person plural, *ils* for males/mixed gender,

If you haven't figured it out, in French, you nearly never say the last syllable. The only case in which you do is if it's followed by a vowel, and even then, there are a lot of exceptions. You'll pick up on this a lot more as you actually work with the language and discover the parameters and tendencies of it. We'll talk more about the difference between *ils* and *elles* momentarily.

On

On is a super important term in French that you're going to run into a lot. It has a direct translation to the English *one*.

When talking to a boss, one says "vous".

Quand parler au patron, on dit << vous >>.

However, it also has an implicit meaning of "we" in reference to an unspecific group.

In France, we drink wine.

En France, on boit le vin.

What's more, in colloquial French, people will often use *on* instead of *nous* in order to avoid the more verbose nous conjugations. Compare the following sentences which mean *we're going to go to the movies*:

On va aller au cinéma. (ohn va AL-ley oh seen-ey-mah, in practice the *va* and *aller* sound like one word: ohn v'AL-ley oh seen-ey-mah)

Nous allons aller au cinéma. (nooz AL-lohn AL-ley oh seen-ey-mah)

The first is much easier to say and remember. This will become far more obvious the more that you work with French and get to more complex conjugations, such as the imperfect tense.

This pronoun deserved its own place because it's very unique and doesn't quite have a direct approximate in English. It is *always* conjugated like the *il/elle* third person pronouns, as it's a third person pronoun itself.

Verb conjugation

Verbs are always conjugated in one way or another. However, English actually has one of the easiest verb conjugation systems of any language. The only thing which makes English verb conjugation particularly difficult is the tendency of it to be irregular and for there to be a lot of verbs to cover terribly specific situations. For example, take the phrase "to wait for". You would think, given the commonness of this particular verb and situation, it would be a verb of its own accord. However, this isn't the case. French, however, *does* have a verb for this - *attendre*. "J'attends mes amis." corresponds to "I'm waiting for my friends."

Anyway, English's verb conjugation is indeed rather simple. However, it still exists in some ways. The normal way that we conjugate regular verbs is to, in the raw indicative form, to add an -s to the third person singular. Like so:

I *eat*, you *eat*, he/she/it *eat***s**, we *eat*, they *eat*.

Or, if it's a present continuous verb, we'll use the auxiliary verb "to be" (which is irregular) before the gerund of the given verb, as we talked about earlier:

I *am eating*, you *are eating*, he/she/it *is eating*, we *are eating*, they *are eating*.

French has a more nuanced system of conjugation than English. There are more endings and forms and even tenses. The saving grace, however, is they tend to follow a pattern all on their own. Once you learn this pattern, verbs become far easier.

The present indicative and the present continuous form a singular tense in French, known simply as the *présent*, which of course means "present". The present can be conjugated in many ways but tends to follow a pattern, as you'll see momentarily.

There are three categories of French verbs: *-re* verbs, *-er* verbs, and *-ir* verbs. Most verbs are *regular*, which means that they follow specific patterns of usage and spelling. There is some contention here, in that quite a few verbs are *irregular*... including the ones which are arguably the most common.

That's not to discourage you at all, though, as even the irregular verbs follow a very similar pattern to the regular verbs. So without further ado, let's conjugate some verbs!

First, we're going to focus on *-er* verbs, with the specific example of *parler*, meaning "to speak".

Parler - *to speak*

Conjugation	Meaning	Pronunciation
Je parl*e*	I speak	Juu pahrl
Tu parl*es*	You speak	Too pahrl
Il/elle/on parl*e*	He/she/it/one speaks	Il/el/ohn pahrl
Nous parl*ons*	We speak	Noo pahr-lohn
Vous parl*ez*	You all/you (f.) speak	Voo pahr-ley
Ils/elles parl*ent*	They speak	Il/el pahrl

The way that conjugation works is by dropping the final two letters of the regular verb, always -er, -ir-, or -re, and replacing them with the given suffix. The suffixes for each pronoun are italicized.

As you can see, the endings for *-er* verbs are *-e*, *-es*, *-e*, *-ons*, *-ez*, and *-ent*.

Now is a better time than any to make a mental note for you: you do NOT pronounce the *-ent* suffix on *-er* verbs. Ever. The verb sounds functionally the same as the third person *singular* conjugation.

Anyway, now let's do an *-ir* verb. The endings for *-ir* verbs are *-is*, *-is*, *-it*, *-issons*, *-issez*, and *-issent*. You don't pronounce the *-ent* here, either. However, it doesn't sound like the third person singular, because the third person singular ends in a *t* sound (if followed by a vowel) or none at all, where the third person plural ends in an *s* sound.

Finir - *to finish*

Conjugation	Meaning	Pronunciation
Je fin*is*	I finish	Juu fee-nee
Tu fin*is*	You finish	Too fee-nee
Il/elle/on fin*it*	He/she/it/one finishes	Il/el/ohn fee-nee
Nous fin*issons*	We finish	Noo fee-nee-sohn
Vous fin*issez*	You all/you (f.) finish	Voo fee-nee-sey
Ils/elles fin*issent*	They finish	Il/el fee-nees

And lastly, we're going to work with regular -re verbs. -Re verbs can be somewhat tricky, because they change the scheme up a bit. The third person singular doesn't add *anything* to the stem. Thus, the -re verb endings are as follows: *-s, -s,* nothing, *-ons, -ez, -ent*. Let's practice this using the verb *vendre*, meaning "to sell".

Vendre - *to sell*

Conjugation	Meaning	Pronunciation
Je vend*s*	I sell	Juu vahnd
Tu vend*s*	You sell	Too vahnd
Il/elle/on vend	He/she/it/one sells	Il/el/ohn vahn
Nous vend*ons*	We sell	Noo vahnd-ohns
Vous vend*ez*	You all/you (f.) sell	Voo vahnd-ey
Ils/elles vend*ent*	They sell	Il/el vahnd

Do you see how this is working? These verbs all follow a very certain manner of spelling, but it certainly does have an order that you can really easily pick up on. And if it seems difficult now, don't worry - it will most definitely make more sense with practice.

I'd like to move onto articles, but we can't quite yet. This is because we need to cover some major *irregular* verbs. These are verbs that you may use which don't follow the same rules as the verbs prior. These are verbs that you'll learn with practice. The first one that we're going to cover is "to be", or *être*. Here's how you conjugate it.

Être - *to be*

Conjugation	Meaning	Pronunciation
Je suis	I am	Juu swee
Tu es	You are	Too ey
Il/elle/on est	He/she/it/one is	Il/el/ohn ey
Nous sommes	We are	Noo sohm
Vous êtes	You all/you (f.) are	Vooz eht
Ils/elles sont	They are	Il/el sohn

You use être pretty much as you would expect to use it. There are certain places where the translation of "to be" don't quite work across English to French, though, but we'll get there in a second.

You use être in order to describe something or somebody, as well as to tell where you are. It actually corresponds largely to "to be" in English, but there are certain cases where it does. For example, in English, we'd say "I'm 20 years old". *Mais en français*, we'd say "I have 20 years". There are a few other examples I'll list off momentarily, after going into the conjugation of "to have".

Avoir - *to have*

Conjugation	Meaning	Pronunciation
J'ai (*Je ai* contraction)	I have	Jey
Tu as	You have	Too ah
Il/elle/on a	He/she/it/one has	Il/el/ohn ah
Nous av*ons*	We have	Noo ah-vohn
Vous av*ez*	You all/you (f.) have	Voo ah-vey
Ils/elles ont	They have	Il/el ohn

So to say *I'm twenty years old* in French, you'd say *j'ai vingt ans* (jey VAHNT ahn) - "I have twenty years".

There are some embarrassing mix-ups between être and avoir which might happen. You need to be mindful and aware of these. Consider, for example, the sentence "I am full". You might be tempted to translate this directly: *je suis plein*. But this is a HORRIBLE idea! Why? Because "*Je suis plein*" *does* mean "I'm full"… as in "I'm full with a baby."

Instead, you'd say **J'ai** plein, or roughly "I have fullness".

This likewise plays out with "I'm hot". If you were to say "Je suis chaude" as a woman, you'd be telling somebody you're *aroused*. Rather, you'd want to say "J'ai chaude" - "I have hot". This means that the temperature is hot, or that you feel an uncomfortable heat.

Avoir is used for a few other phrases similarly to describe personal feelings. *J'ai faim* would mean "I'm hungry", though it literally means *I have hunger*.

The next verb we have to cover is *faire*. *Faire* technically means "to do" or "to make", but it has a ton of idiomatic expressions as well. Here's how you conjugate faire:

Faire - *to do, to make*

Conjugation	Meaning	Pronunciation
Je fais	I do, I make	Juu feh
Tu fais	You do, you make	Too feh
Il/elle/on fait	He/she/it/one does, he/she/it/one makes	Il/el/ohn feh
Nous fais*ons*	We do, we make	Noo feh-zohn
Vous faites	You all/you (f.) do, you all/you (f.) make	Voo feht
Ils/elles font	They do, they make	Il/el fohn

There are many cases where you'll use "faire", like so.

Où est Timothie? (Where is Timothy?)

*Dans sa chambre. Il **fait** <u>ses devoirs</u>*. (He's in his room. He's *doing* **his homework**.)

It's also has quite a few idiomatic uses. For example, if it's a nice day out, you would say "*Il fait beau*" - literally "It's doing handsome". If it's hot, you'd say "*il fait chaud*" and if it's cold, you'd say "*il fait froid*". In other words, if you're using an adjective to describe the weather, you'd use *il fait...* before it. However, if you're describing a current weather action, like rain or snow, you use the verb for those: *neiger* and *pleuvoir* specifically. "It's snowing" would be "Il neige" (Il nehj) and "It's raining" would be "Il pleut" (Il ploo).

Another verb that we need to cover is *aller*, which means "to go". You need to understand this verb in order to understand the near future tense later.

Aller - *to go*

Conjugation	Meaning	Pronunciation
Je vais	I go	Juu vey
Tu vas	You go	Too vah
Il/elle/on va	He/she/it/one goes	Il/el/ohn vah
Nous all*ons*	We go	Nooz al-LOHN
Vous allez	You all/you (p.) go	Vooz al-LEY
Ils/elles vont	They go	Il/el vohn

You would use *aller* exactly as you'd expect to. If you're going to a place, you of course would use a preposition to denote it. The preposition is generally à:

Je vais à la bibliothèque. (juu vey-z-ah lah beeb-leeh-oh-tek)

I'm going to the library.

We'll talk more about à in the chapter regarding prepositions, though.

There's one more irregular verb I'm going to specifically hop into in this chapter before we head into the next one about the wonderfully confusing world of French pronunciation: *venir*, or "to come". The cool thing about *venir* is that once you understand it, you understand the verbs which spring from it - *revenir*, meaning "to come back/come again"; *devenir*, meaning "to become"; *souvenir*, meaning "to remember". Here's how you would conjugate *venir* and its derivatives:

Venir - *to come*

Conjugation	Meaning	Pronunciation

Je viens	I come	Juu vee-ahn
Tu viens	You come	Too vee-ahn
Il/elle/on vient	He/she/it/one comes	Il/el/ohn vee-ahn
Nous venons	We come	Noo vuu-nohn
Vous venez	You all/you (p.) come	Voo vuu-ney
Ils/elles viennent	They come	Il/el vee-ehn

Venir is often paired with "de", meaning "from" or "of". Observe:

D'où viens-tu? ("Where are you from?", literally "from where are you coming?")

Je viens des États-Unis. ("I come from the United States.")

There are a few more big verbs, but we'll cover them later on in the book. For now, just try to get some practice with -er, -ir, and -re verbs. I've included some regular -er, -ir, and -re verbs in order to help you get the hang of it through practice and dedication.

insert verbs

Articles

Before we move on to the next chapter, it's absolutely necessary that we cover articles. Articles make up a huge part of French. Every single noun must have an article before it, no exceptions. Well, some exceptions, but they're very few.

What are articles? They're not what you read in the paper or on Facebook, shared by a zealous family member. No, *articles* are the part of speech which refers to the marker for a noun. That is to say, look at the following sentences:

*I eat **some** apples.*

*I eat **the** apples.*

*I eat **an** apple.*

Some, the, and *an* are the markers here, because they tell you the specificity of the thing. *Some* means that you're eating any given apples. *The* implies that you're eating a very specific, previously referenced set of apples. *An* implies that you eat any given apple.

In French, this is expanded upon, much like verb conjugation.

Before we talk about that, we need to talk about *gendered nouns*. Every noun in French has a gender. This doesn't mean that an *apple* is a woman, of course. It's not going to bear your child or anything. The genders of nouns are a totally grammatical separation - a holdover from Vulgar Latin, more or less. The genders are also intrinsic to French. A lot of words would be a lot weirder and a lot of phraseologies would be a lot stranger if gendered nouns were slowly phased out.

The idea of gendered nouns may seem extremely bizarre to an English speaker, and indeed, it can be a little strange at first. None of our nouns have genders. But after practice and dedication, you'll start to learn what makes a noun a certain gender and be able to more or less guess what gender a noun is with some degree of accuracy.

It's important to note that the gender of a noun will correlate to it in subject pronouns, like so:

"Comment tu l'aimes, la pomme?" (How do you like the apple?)

"Elle est un peu acide." (It's a tad tart.)

"Apple" is feminine - *la pomme* - and so when we reference it in the sentence following, we have to use the feminine pronoun.

Anyhow, back to the main topic of articles.

Firstly, we have *definite articles*. These correspond to "the". There are four different definite articles:

Le - masculine singular: *Le pont* ("the bridge")

La - feminine singular: *La vache* ("the cow")

Les - plural: *Les enfants* ("the children")

L' - followed by vowel: *L'art* ("the art")

You use definite articles when you're talking about a specific instance of something. Basically, in the same way that you'd use "the" in English. You also use it when you're referring to something in a broader sense, where in English we'd normally *drop* the article altogether.

For example, if you wanted to say "I like oranges", you'd use the definite articles - *J'aime les oranges* - where in English we don't use an article at all in that sentence.

After definite articles, we have *partitive* articles. These basically mean "some of" or "any". These are as follows:

Du - masculine singular: *Du vin* ("some wine")

De la - feminine singular: *De la pizza* ("some pizza")

Des - plural: *Des framboises* ("some raspberries")

De l' - before vowel: *De l'eau* ("some water")

Generally, partitive articles are used in reference to food or drink.

The last form of article in French is the *indefinite* article. This correlates to "a" or "an" in English. This has two forms:

Un - masculine singular: *Un léon* ("A lion")

Une - feminine singular: *Une langue* ("A language")

That about sums up articles in French. We can go a bit further with them, but that involves the next part, which is…

Negation

Okay, I lied. There's actually one more major thing we have to cover before we go onto the next part. That's the concept of "negation". Negation means simply taking something and then turning it negative. We negative things in English by adding "do not". For example:

"I don't like to walk."

"He doesn't talk."

"We don't look."

You can also negate things in French. You do so by surrounding the verb with *ne pas*. The *ne* indicates a negative statement, where the *pas* means specifically "not".

So to take those sentences we just wrote and translate them:

"Je **n'**aime **pas** marcher." (Juu nehm pah mahr-chey)

"Il **ne** parle **pas**." (Il nuu pahrl pah)

"Nous/on **ne** regardons/regarde **pas**." (Noo/ohn nuu ruu-gahr-dohn/ruu-gahrd pah)

See how that works?

Now, how do articles come into play? Well, if you have a negative statement, it's important to take note that the article will change if you're negating a sentence with partitive or indefinite articles. However, it doesn't change in sentences with definite articles.

Here's a sentence with an indefinite article:

J'ai une plume. (I have a pen.)

And here it is, negated:

Je n'ai pas de plume. (I don't have a pen.)

This change, however, does *not* occur in sentences with definite articles.

*As-tu vu **le** film? (Have you seen the film?)*

*Non, je n'ai vu **le** film. (No, I haven't seen the film.)*

While we're on the topic of negation, there are a few special cases where you *don't* use "ne...pas", and where "pas" actually changes.

These are as follows:

Ne...rien	-	"nothing"
Ne...jamais	-	"never"
Ne...pas encore	-	"not yet"
Ne...plus	-	"not any longer"
Ne...personne	-	"nobody"

So you could use these as follows:

Je ne veux rien. ("I want nothing," or "I don't want anything.")

Il ne le fait pas encore. ("He hasn't done it yet.")

Nous ne sommes contents plus. ("We aren't happy anymore.")

They're a little obtuse to learn and understand at first, but they're not too terribly difficult to grasp once you get the hang of them, and they can make your writing far more expressive, too.

Chapter 2: Pronunciation

French is a beast when it comes to pronunciation. I'm not even going to lie to you, not for a second. The hardest thing when it came to learning French for me, starting out, was listening and speaking. Reading and writing French can be a breeze once you grasp the finer points, but actually making sense of the bizarre syllabary, that's another story entirely. It can be really difficult coming from a language like English to understand all of the nuances of French pronunciation. But luckily, I'm here to try to help you through the major parts.

Liaison

The first topic we're going to cover is *liaison*. This is the idea of connecting sounds. It's part of what makes French such a beautiful and graceful language to listen to.

Somewhere along the line during the development of French, the final pronunciation of letters in words dropped for the most part. However, there are certain locations where these letters can still be heard.

Take, for example, the article *les*. By itself, it's boring - it sounds like "lay", and you don't pronounce the *s*. However, if we put a word with a vowel in front of it, like *éléphants* ("elephants", of course), the *s* in *les* is heard:

J'aime bien les éléphants. (Jehm bee-ahn lay-z-ey-ley-fahn-t)
I really like/quite like the elephants.

This is a super important concept to nail. It can be rather difficult to ascertain and follow through with at first. I remember that when I started out in French, this concept absolutely *floored* me. I had no idea what to do with this or how to apply it. After all, French spellings can often be so weird anyway - how was I supposed to remember when one is supposed to insert a consonant you wouldn't normally hear?

Well, it's a natural fear, and as with most fears, it turned out to be rather unfounded. With time and practice, I found myself to naturally pick up liaison.

There are some very specific cases for liaison, however - and some places you never use it.

Generally, you use liaison if the word preceding the vowel ends in either an *l, t, d, p, s, f, and x*. They generally sound as you'd expect, except for *f* which sounds like a *v*, *d* which sounds like a *t*, and *x* which sounds like an *s*.

There are three kinds of liaison in French: *required*, *forbidden*, and *optional*.

Required liaison exist in many different cases. You *have* to use liaison with these words, there is not an option as to whether you do or not. These words are generally words which are linked in some way or another. You'll use this type of liaison after pronouns (*nous allons*), between a number and a noun (*trois amis*), after prepositions which have only one preposition (*en avance*), after articles (*un orange*), after *est*, after *comment* when asking someone how they're doing (*comment allez-vous?*), between a preceding adjective and its respective noun (*bon homme*), and after monosyllabic adverbs (*très horrible*).

Then, there are *forbidden* liaison. No matter what, you don't use the liaison in these cases. You will never, ever use liaison *before* or *after* somebody's name, after et, before the word *onze* (*J'avais onze ans*), before the word "oui" (*Je lui dis "oui"*), after any sort of plural nouns, before the preposition à, after any sort of singular noun, or before an H wherein you actually *say* the h. (These don't come up often in French, though - the H is *usually* silent.)

Then, there are optional liaisons. These are liaisons which you may or may not say. There is no rule regarding these. These pop up because language is always shifting around and modifying itself throughout time. If you encounter a liaison which is out of the realm of the formerly discussed ones, it's safe to say it's an optional liaison.

French vowels

The next major thing to talk about is the French vowels. These are relatively finite compared to English vowels, but can trip you up if you don't know them. There are also more *exact* vowel sounds because the French alphabet has accents, where the English alphabet does not.

Let's start from the beginning, shall we?

a - pronounced as an "ah"
à - pronounced as an "ah"
â - pronounced as a long "ah"
e - middle of a syllable, like "eh"; end of a syllable, like "uu"
é - pronounced like "ay"
ê - pronounced like "eh"
i - pronounced like "ee"
o - pronounced like "oh"
ô - pronounced like "oh" - denotes where a letter has been dropped in the past.
u - there's no comparable English sound; say "eeh" but then round your lips as though you're saying "ooh". The resulting sound is the French *u*.
y - pronounced like "ee"

Then, there are some really important diphthongs you need to remember.

(A diphthong is a combination of two vowels in order to form a new sound.)

ai - pronounced like "eh"
au - pronounced like "oh"
eau - pronounced like "oh"
ei - pronounced like "eh"
eu - pronounced like "uu"
oeu - pronounced like "uu"
oi - pronounced like "wah"
ou - pronounced like "ooh"

French vowels are easy and relatively simple to understand, so long as you practice. Now onto the consonants.

French consonants

The consonants, you most likely know. Here are the ones which aren't so consistent with English and may trip you up.

c - before an e or an i, it will sound like an s; in any other place, it will sound like the "c" in "cool"
ç - will sound like an s always
ch - will sound like the 'sh' in 'shoe'
g - before an e or an i, it will sound like the *s* in the word "pleasure"; in any other place, it sounds like the English g.
h - normally silent
j - sounds like the French g
qu - sounds like the "c" in "cool"
s - sounds normal if at the beginning, but like a z if in the middle of two vowels.

Using these tips, you should be able to irk out French words with little difficulty.

Chapter 3: Past and Future Tenses

French is a rather easy language to learn, but the hardest thing about it when you're coming from an English speaking background is most certainly its numerous convoluted verb tenses.

There are *at least four* basic French past tenses, and just as many basic French future tenses. You can get away with, at the basic level, knowing just two of the French past tenses, and just two of the French future tenses.

Let's take these one at a time.

Passé composé

Passé composé literally means *compound past*, and is the most common past tense used in French. It's used to reference an action which has been completed at the time of speaking, or at some point in the past. It's a relatively simple tense to form.

The passé composé is made up of two parts: the *auxiliary verb*, and the *past participle*. The auxiliary verb is *normally* avoir, but it can also be être (more on that momentarily). The *past participle* is the past tense form of the word. For example, if "I'm eating" is the present continuous, then "I have eaten" is the past perfect, wherein *have* is the auxiliary verb and *eaten* is the past participle. French works similarly.

So how do you form the past participle? It's simple.

For **-ir** verbs, you drop the **-ir** and replace it with an **-i**. *Finir*, for example, would be *fini*.

For **-er** verbs, you drop the **-er** and replace it with an **-é**. Thus, *manger* would become *mangé*.

For **-re** verbs, you drop the **-re** and replace it with an **-u**. Thus, *vendre* would become *vendu*.

To form the passé composé, all you do is conjugate the auxiliary verb to the person speaking (normally *avoir*), and then get the past participle. So "I have eaten" in French would become "J'ai mangé". "He has sold the strawberries" would be "Il a vendu les fraises".

Simple enough, right? Now the question becomes "when do we use être as opposed to avoir?"

Well, there's actually a system for this: just remember DR. and MRS. VANDERTRAMP. Seriously. That's the mnemonic.

When you're using *intransitive* verbs which indicate either motion (going somewhere) or a change of state (changing in some essential way), you use *être* as your auxiliary verb.

The following are the verbs which will use être:

Devenir - to become something
Rentrer - to enter something again
Monter - to go up something (e.g., stairs)
Rester - to stay
Sortir - to leave, exit, or go out
Venir - to come
Aller - to go somewhere
Naître - to be born to somebody
Descendre - to go down something or descend
Entrer - to enter into something
Retourner - to return to something
Tomber - to fall down or trip
Revenir - to return to something or to come back
Arriver - to arrive to/at something
Mourir - to die
Partir - to leave somewhere

An important thing to note about using être as an auxiliary verb is that you must adjust the passé composé to match the gender and person. So "he left" would be "il est venu", but "she left" would be "elle est venue", and "they left" would be "ils sont venus".

This, however, is not the case when you're using *avoir* as the auxiliary verb. When using *avoir*, the subject and the participle need not agree. The past participle of avoir must, however, agree with the direct object pronoun if it's present before the verb. (More on that momentarily.)

Imparfait

So we talked about the most common French past tense. But there's another incredibly important one that we have yet to cover at all. This tense is known as the *imparfait*. The *imparfait*, or "imperfect", doesn't refer at all to a completed event. Rather, it refers to a given ongoing event or state in the past ("I was happy", "I was young") or a repeated event ("I used to watch..."). This concept doesn't have a direct correlative in English, but the English tense "past continuous" or "past progressive" can certainly get across the same exact point.

The imperfect is simple to form.

For **-er** and **-re** verbs, you just drop the ending and add *-ais, -ais, -ait, -ions, -iez,* or *-aient*.

For **-ir** verbs, you do the same, but you add an "iss" before it.

So for example, if you wanted to say "When I was young, I would play often.", you would say "*Quand j'**étais** jeune, je **jouais** souvent.*"

The imperfect is notoriously difficult to master, but it will come in handy quite often for you, so it's worth teaching anyway.

These are the main cases in which you'd want to use the imperfect over the passé composé:

- Actions or states which occurred often and not just once
- Descriptions of either emotional or physical states: personal feelings, one's age, the given time and weather.
- Any states or actions where the duration is ongoing but unknown.
- Used alongside the passé composé in order to give more depth or information.
- Polite suggestion and wishes - "Pourrais-tu m'aider?" : "Could you help me?" (literally "Would you have the ability to give me help?")
- As part of a conditional clause.

Futur Proche

Futur proche literally means "close future" and refers to events which will most certainly happen, and soon. The futur proche is insanely easy to create. All that you do is combine *aller* (to go) conjugated to the person alongside the infinitive of the verb to be carried out in the near future.

Je vais faire les magasins.
"I'm going to go shopping."

Ils vont jouer au basket.
"They're going to go play basketball."

You can combine this, of course, with dates or times to explicitly state when an action is going to be undertaken.

Vas-tu aller à la librairie demain?
"Are you going to the bookstore tomorrow?"

This is, of course, a very simple tense, but you'll find it incredibly useful. When you're out and about and scratching surface-type conversations with native French speakers, it's unlikely that as a tourist or newcomer, you're going to need to tell them your grand far-future life goals. However, if you need to, that's what the next tense is for.

Futur Simple

The *simple future* tense is, well, simple. It's a very no-nonsense tense that is a little more complicated than the previous tense, and it can be quite easy to sound like you have no idea what you're talking about. However, it's worth learning anyway, because it's a rather common tense.

The futur simple just implies something that will happen at some point in the future. The way that you form it is by taking the *entire infinitive* of a verb as the stem, and then adding *-ai, -as, -a, -ons, -ez,* or *-ont* depending upon who is talking. If the verb ends in **-re**, then and only then do you remove something from the verb, taking off the final -e before adding your ending.

Note that some verbs are irregular, such as être and avoir. These have the future stems of *ser-* and *aur-*, respectively.

So let's try this with the verb *chanter*, meaning "to sing". Here's how we'd do it:

Chanter - *to sing, futur simple*

Conjugation	Meaning	Pronunciation
Je chanter*ai*	I will sing	Juu shahn-teh-reh
Tu chanter*as*	You will sing	Too shahn-teh-rah
Il/elle/on chanter*a*	He/she/it/one will sing	Il/el/ohn shahn-teh-rah
Nous chanter*ons*	We will sing	Noo shahn-teh-rohn
Vous chanter*ez*	You all/you (p.) will sing	Voo shahn-teh-rey
Ils/elles chanter*ont*	They will sing	Il/el shahn-teh-rohn

Simple enough, right? The futur simple isn't a terribly difficult tense to use in and of itself, and it's rather easy to set up.

You are halfway done!

Congratulations on making it to the halfway point of the journey. Many try and give up long before even getting to this point, so you are to be congratulated on this. You have shown that you are serious about getting better every day. I am also serious about improving my life, and helping others get better along the way. To do this I need your feedback. Click on the link below and take a moment to let me know how this book has helped you. If you feel there is something missing or something you would like to see differently, I would love to know about it. I want to ensure that as you and I improve, this book continues to improve as well. Thank you for taking the time to ensure that we are all getting the most from each other.

Chapter 4: Questions and Objects

We're going to knock out two seemingly unrelated birds with one very big stone in this chapter. In French, questions and objects actually intertwine in a way. I suppose that they intertwine in any given language, really. In a lot of conversations, you'll be talking about a given subject, and in order to carry on the conversation, you'll find it necessary to ask questions about what the other person is saying. So questions like "When did you see it?" or "How did you get in there?" or "How was it?" will naturally crop up.

That is to say that any budding French conversationalist will need both of these concepts quite handily, and I'm prepared to set you up with them.

Questions

French questions are rather easy. Every question is composed of question words. Much like in English, every proper question has a word which designates *what* exactly we're asking about.

In English, these words are *what, why, how, with whom, who, which, how many*, and *where*.

In French, the words are as follows:

Quoi - What
Quand - When
Pourquoi - Why
Quel(le)(s) - Which
Combien de - How many
Comment - How
Où - Where
Qui - Who
Avec qui - With whom

These, of course, function just like they do in English - they can be parts of normal statements, or they can be used in questions.

If used in questions, there's another phrase you need to know: *est-ce que* (pronounced EST kuu). This literally translate to "is it that?". When combined with other question words, or on its own, it signals that the statement following it is a question.

Est-ce que tu l'aimes?
Do you love him?
(literally "is it [the case] that you love him?")

Où est-ce que tu chantes?
Where do you sing?
(literally "Where is it that you sing?")

This phrase already is powerful, but sometimes you don't want such a clunky phrase. Sometimes, in fact, you can say more with less. This is when inverted questions become the go-to.

And indeed, they're a little familiar to us as English speakers. Think of it this way: let's say you walked into your living room wanting to watch a certain show, but your brother or child was there watching TV, though absentmindedly since they're also playing on their DS and seem mostly preoccupied with that. You want to change the channel. What do you do?

Well, so long as you aren't a barbarian, you'll normally ask something along the lines of:
Are you watching the TV?

Which is an inverted question. What if you just wanted to say that they were watching TV? You would instead say:
You are watching the TV.

So the "you" and the "are" were inverted in order to make the sentence into a question. French questions work similarly to this mechanism.

Let's say the same scenario happened. With the little est-ce que trick we just learned, we might be tempted to say this:
Est-ce que tu regardes la télé?

But we can make this a lot shorter and snappier. We can just invert the question:
Regardes-tu la télé?

This kind of inversion will serve you very well and explain a lot of potentially confusing sentences you'll run into.

Direct object pronouns

This is a really tedious but very necessary lesson to give. We use direct object pronouns *constantly*. Think about it: have you ever been talking about something with a friend, and then you something like "Yeah, I saw them" or "Yeah, I heard it."? The answer, of course, is yes. It would be incredibly monotonous, slightly robotic, and ultimately very creepy if we *didn't* have direct object pronouns. It would feel absolutely unnatural to say the name of something every time we brought it up. Of course, it wouldn't if that were just the way we spoke, but from *our perspective* and speaking *the way we do*, it sounds odd. Besides, it saves time. Replacing a multi-syllable name or phrase with the simple "it" or "them" or "him" saves a lot of time and effort in terms of speaking and writing.

So how do direct object pronouns in French work? Well, I'm assuming that you know how they work in English already.

In French, you correlate the previously mentioned object to the correct direct object pronoun based on perspective (is it first person? second person? third person?) and plurality (singular? plural?). Then you just throw it before the noun. (Notice how I just said "throw *it* before the noun" -- direct object pronouns at work!)

The French direct object pronouns are as follows:
me - first person singular
te - second person singular
le, **la**, **l'** - third person singular
nous - first person plural
vous - second person plural
les - third person plural

So let's say that I wanted to say "I'm giving *it* to Jeffrey." How would I do so?

Well, I first recognize the "direct object". Here, it's *it*. Then I analyze to see which word fits it: *it* refers to a singular third person object, so I'll use the third person singular. Then, we have to figure out the gender of the noun. Let's say we're giving Jeffrey a papaya. This translates to *une papaye*, which is feminine. So it's a feminine third person singular direct object. Perfect. The word is *la*.

So to say "I'm giving it to Jeffrey", knowing "it" is *la*, I just have to translate the rest, and throw the *la* before the verb, like so:

Je la donne à Jeffrey.

Honestly, explaining it makes it sound so much more difficult than it really is. In practice, it's a very easy concept to grasp and there's not a whole lot of genuine difficulty involved in it.

Indirect object pronouns

This is where it gets a bit trickier. There's a huge difference between direct object pronouns and indirect object pronouns. The *direct* object is the object which is directly affected by a given verb. The *indirect* object is the object which receives the brunt of the action of the verb.

The way I like to put it is this: without the *direct object*, there is no *verb*. Full stop. If you throw a ball, you can't *detach* the ball from the concept of *throwing*. Either you're throwing a ball, or there is nothing to be thrown. The same with sending a letter. You can't just *send nothing*. You have to have something to *be* sending. You can absolutely *not* detach the concept of the letter from the notion of *sending*.

However, this is where indirect objects are different. You can detach the indirect object from the rest. The indirect object is non-essential. You can throw a ball without throwing it *to* somebody. You can send a letter without sending it *to* somebody (though it may not go anywhere.) You can do these things *without* the existence of the indirect object. But since the indirect object is *there*, it serves to give context to the verb and the direct object, by giving them an end goal and, indeed, a thing for which and to which they're performed.

The French indirect object pronouns are as follows:

me - *to me*
te - *to you*
lui - *to him/to her*
nous - *to us*
vous - *to you all/to you (f.)*
leur - to them

So let's go back to that sentence from the direct object pronoun section: "I'm giving it to Jeffrey". We ended up getting the following:

Je la donne à Jeffrey.

So how do we get the indirect object pronoun here? We first find the preposition, which will indicate to/for whom or what the action is being performed. The preposition here is à, and the prepositional phrase is "à Jeffrey." Thus, the indirect object is Jeffrey. So that's a third person singular indirect object, and it's gender neutral in the indirect object form, so we can just take *lui* and stick it behind our verb too.

Je la lui donne.

This literally means "I'm giving it to him." Not too shabby, no?

The general rule for placement of direct and indirect object pronouns, when you have both, is that they go in alphabetical order.

Adverbial pronouns

There are a couple of other pronouns you need to be aware of. They are as follows:

y - replaces "there"; also replaces "à" and a noun.

en - replaces either a partitive article and noun ("Je mange des pommes" becomes "J'en mange") or replaces *de* followed by an indefinite article and a noun ("J'ai envie d'une plume" becomes "J'en ai envie") which makes it particularly useful for shortening phrases of verbs which traditionally are followed by de (*se souvenir de* - to be reminded of, *avoir besoin de* - to need, *avoir envie de* - to want, and so on...)

These are called *adverbial pronouns*, and will turn out to be quite useful as you go forward with French. You'll understand the usage of them more as you practice with them and read/hear more and more French.

Ce, cela, celui, and so on

One of the most important French phrases you'll ever encounter is *c'est* (sey). It's somewhat of a catchall. For example, "C'est mon chien !" means "This is/that is/it is my dog!". "Ça, c'est mon ami, [name]" can be used to introduce one friend to another. "Ça, c'est intéressant!" means "That's interesting!". The French have such a love affair with "ça, c'est" that they'll use it places where it really doesn't belong, but you'll figure that out on your own.

C'est is a contraction of the pronoun *ce* and the verb *est*. It means approximately "it is", "this is", or "that is" depending upon the context. "Ce" just means "this" or "that". You can use it before a noun, too, to indicate a specific one. For example, "ce chien" means *this dog*. If you do this, you have to pay attention to your spelling. If it's used before a masculine noun with a vowel, you have to use *cet* instead of *ce*. If it's before a feminine noun, you must use *cette*. If it's before a plural noun, you must use *ces*.

There are some other forms, too. *Ceci* and *cela* are important for you to know - they both mean approximately "this" and "that", but can be used somewhat interchangeably. Cela contracts to the popular *ça*.

Then, there's *celui* and *celle*. *Celle* is the feminine form of *celui*. They both mean "this one" or "that one" dependent upon context, and refer to one of a specific group of different people or things in a given set.

These are important pronouns for you to know just because they're so prolific in French usage.

Chapter 5: Adjectives, Adverbs, Conjunctions, and Prepositions

Before we get to the conversational pillars of French, we need to talk about some major parts of speech.

Adjectives

Adjectives are a huge part of speaking any language. They allow you to describe nouns and objects. French adjectives are relatively easy for the most part. However, their only tricky asset is that the vast majority of them have to match their respective objects which they describe in terms of plurality and gender. This can make for quite a mess when you're newer to French.

Take, for example, the French adjective *joli*, meaning "pretty" or "cute". If I wanted to say "He is pretty", I would say "Il est joli". However, if I wanted to say "she is pretty", I would instead say "Elle est joli*e*". Notice the addition of the *e* to make it feminine.

Depending upon what exactly the adjective is, there are different ways to make one feminine. For example, the vast majority of adjectives can be made feminine simply by the addition of an *-e* to the end of it.

A key difference between English and French adjectives is that French adjectives nearly always go *after* the noun in question, which can really trip you up at first. After a while, it starts to make sense in its own way - after all, it's just another manner of communication. However, avoid falling into the trap of accidentally using an adjective incorrectly because you don't know any better.

Some adjectives *do* go before the noun though. It can be hard to remember which ones exactly, but just think of the following acronym: *beauty, age, goodness, size*. Adjectives which have to do with those typically can go before the adjective rather than after.

Additionally, you very much need to be wary of the meanings of your adjectives. Certain adjectives can go before *and* after a noun. However, this can create two diametrically different meanings depending upon the placement. Take, for example, *curieux*.

If you place *curieux* before the noun, it means weird or strange. However, if you place it after the noun, it means curious or inquisitive. In other words, the correct adjective placement can be the difference between giving praise to your kid and calling them a total weirdo. Be more careful than to call your kid a total weirdo, my friend.

Adverbs

Adverbs describe verbs and adjectives. Adverbs are incredibly easy to form. You may notice a parallel between French adverbs and Spanish adverbs if you've spent any time study Spanish, by chance: you form adverbs by taking the adjective you'd like to make into an adverb, putting it into its feminine form, and appending *ment* to it, similar to how you form adverbs in Spanish.

Take, for example, the adjective *lent*, meaning slow. Now, let's put it in its feminine form, which gives us *lente*. Then, we just add *ment*, the French equivalent of the English "-ly", and we've got *lentement* meaning *slowly*. In a sentence:

"Parleriez-vous lentement? Je ne parle pas bien français." ("Would you speak slowly? I don't speak French well.")

Overall, the process of creating adverbs in French is super easy.

Conjunctions

Conjunctions are an integral part of any language. I say this because we haven't talked about them at all, yet there's not really a part of language which is dedicated to providing logical order to sentences so much as the conjunctions are.

There are quite a few conjunctions in the French language. More than quite a few, actually. There are a ton of them. Let's start with the coordinating conjunctions. What coordinating conjunctions are are conjunctions that serve to connect two different clauses without placing some sort of emphasis on one or the other. In French, there are actually seven different coordinating conjunctions.

Mais - but
Et - and
Ou - or
Or - now
Ni - neither, nor (used in pairs)
Parce que - because
Donc - thus, so

These all have their own particular uses, and you can likely figure out approximately how to use them based off of their English translations. Indeed, basing their usage off of their English translations is a relatively safe way to use these powerful parts of speech.

Next, there are *subordinating* conjunctions. These are a bit more complicated to use, so if something a little weird, I'll put an example by it in parentheses.

Comme - like, as, since (*Il est courageux comme le léon - he is courageous like the lion*)
Quand - when
Lorsque - when
Que - that (*Je sais bien que tu as raison - I know for certain that you're right.*)
Si - if

And then there are just some general ones that you need to know:

Avant que - before the event of (*Je suis parti avant qu'elle est arrivée. - I left before she arrived.*)
Autant que - to the extent that
Bien que - although
Tel(le)(s) que - such that

This is just scratching the surface, really. There are absurd amounts of French conjunctions out there. But with the knowledge that I've given you thus far, you should be able to make your way around moderately well.

Prepositions

We've already learned a couple of prepositions in French, such as à (meaning to, at, or in) and de (meaning of or from). However, there are even more that we haven't talked about! A lot of these things which have relatively direct English translations, but others are ones which will take a bit more explanation. Let's dive in.

à cause de - thanks to (negative)
à travers - through
après - after
au lieu de - instead of something
avant - before
avec - with
chez - *chez* is a tricky one. It can mean "at the location of *x* person's house", where chez moi means "at my home" or "to my home"; it can also mean "at a company's name" as in "J'ai mangé chez McDonald's"; lastly, it can simply mean "for" - "Quel marche chez toi?" meaning "What worked for you?"
contre - against something
dans - in (used if followed by article)
depuis - since, for (in reference to a length of time)
dès - ever since
en - in (used if not followed by article)
entre - between
environ - approximately
grâce à - thanks to (positive)
jusqu'à - up to, until

par - by, before, alongside, through
pendant - during, for (in reference to a length of time)
pour - for
sous - under
sur - on
vers - towards something, but also to say "around" when talking about numbers

Those are a ton of prepositions to hopefully get you started. You need to be using a lot of this to the extent that you can. Be writing to yourself in private journals and things of the like; try your hand at reading online news and forums. Work with what you've learned.

Chapter 6: Conversational Necessities

So you've landed in France or Quebec and wherever, and you've got a working knowledge of the *mechanics* of French. But *oupsie*, you've got no clue how to have a conversation. What do we do here?

Well, I'll admit, I waited until the last chapter to teach you to have a French conversation because otherwise, you'd just be doing the tourist-y thing of learning several words and phrases without learning *how* they work or *why* they work. And I'll be honest, you'll have a much easier time communicating in France or Quebec if you know how the language works, because the tourist-y phrases hardly make any sense from a linguistic standpoint.

Anyhow, I'll walk you through a French conversation, perhaps with an acquaintance or perhaps with someone new.

The first thing you're going to want to do, of course, is say hello. There are a lot of ways that you can do this in French.

First, if it's in the morning or afternoon, you could say *bonjour*. If it's the evening, you could say *bonsoir*.

This is very formal though. In less formal situations, perhaps around people you know, say *Salut!* instead. (sah-loo) You could also get away with saying *Hé!*

And of course, if you're answering the phone, you say *Allô*. (ah-loh) This is equivalent to the English "hello?" on the phone, and carries the same weight.

If you're wanting to welcome people, you'd say "Bienvenue!". (bee-ahn-vuu-noo)

Anyhow, now you've said hello. What do you do?

Well, you could ask the person a little bit about how they're doing. If they're a stranger, your best bet is to say "Comment allez-vous?" which means "How are you doing?" It's the formal phrase, and can be used with strangers as well as the elderly and your higher-ups in school and work. If you know the person a bit better, you might say "Comment ça va?" (coh-mohn sah vah) or "Comment vas-tu?" (coh-mohn vah tue)

Let's say that you want to get to know them. You may say "Qu'est-ce que tu aimes faire?" or "qu'est-ce que vous aimez faire?" depending upon the formality of the situation, both meaning "What do you like to do?"

Or maybe you're younger and trying to find out how old someone about your age is. In that case, you could just say "Tu as quel âge?", literally meaning

"You have what age?"

Finally, it's going to eventually come to be time to end the conversation, sadly. At that point, there are a couple different ways in which you could say goodbye.

The first is **au revoir**, meaning simply "until we meet again". Pronounced oh ruu-vwah, it's useful in most any situation, formal or informal.

Then, there is **à plus tard** (ah plue tar) which means "see you later", but this is purely informal. You may hear this as "à plus" (ah plues).

Next up is **à bientôt** (ah bee-ehn-toh) which means "see you soon". You can use this formally, as well as informally.

Also useful is **à la prochaine** (ah lah pro-shehn), which means "until next time". Use this when you don't know when you're going to see the other person.

À demain (ah duu-mahn) can mean "see you tomorrow".

Last is **adieu**, which is the most final goodbye. You only use this when you know you'll never see somebody again. If the French hit one nail on the head every time, it's dramaticism.

To spare you from the cheesy explanations from everything, I'm now just going to put some really useful phrases that you're probably going to end up using at one time or another in your journey. I hope the context and background I've given you serves you well in understanding them and there usage:

S'il te plaît/s'il vous plaît - *Please.*
Je voudrais [...] - *I would like [...]*
Je prends [...] - *I'll have [...]*
Merci. - *Thank you.*
Je m'appelle [...] - *My name is [...]*
Comment est [...] - *How is the [...] ? / What's [...] like?*
D'accord. - *Okay.*
Je ne sais pas. - *I don't know.*
Je n'ai aucune idée. - *I have no idea.*
De rien. - *You're welcome.*
Pas de problème. - *No problem.*
Pas de soucis. - *Don't worry.*
Je ne te comprends pas. - *I'm not understanding you.*
Comment dit-on [...] en français? - *How do you say [...] in French?*
Qu'est-ce que ça va dire, [...] ? - *What does [...] mean?*
Combien coûte-t-il? - *How much does it cost?*

Conclusion

Thank for making it through to the end of **_Learn French_** let's hope it was informative and able to provide you with all of the tools you need to achieve your goals whatever they may be.

The next step is to go further with all of this. I've given you the essential grammatical knowledge, but the trade-off of teaching you so much so briskly is that I didn't give you as much in-depth knowledge regarding vocabulary as I would have liked to. This works out in your favor, though - I encourage you to use Duolingo in order to build your vocabulary. This is because where free online services fail is where I've succeeded. I've tried to give you a firm *grammatical* basis of French, that way when you do learn vocab, you know precisely how to use it. Duolingo and services as such are great for memorizing vocab, but don't do so hot when it comes to giving you the practical knowledge of application.

By using the combination of the two - my technical knowledge of the language and the great reference book I've left you with, and the immense focus of Duolingo on vocabulary, you'll be set straight for success and will have an awe-inspiring grasp of the language in no time.

You can also use the site ankisrs.net in order to put the vocab that you've learned into flash cards. You can use this online flash cards utility in order to hone your ability to speak French like a champion.

I genuinely hope that over the course of this book, I've managed to set you up for success. I fully believe that I have, but the proof will be in the pudding of you learning and applying French in your day to day life. I fully expect that you can do that.

Finally, if you found this book useful in anyway, a review on Amazon is always appreciated!

Enjoy yourself, and every second that you spend learning this beautiful language.

Help me improve this book

While I have never met you, if you made it through this book I know that you are the kind of person that is wanting to get better and is willing to take on tough feedback to get to that point. You and I are cut from the same cloth in that respect. I am always looking to get better and I wish to not just improve myself, but also this book. If you have positive feedback, please take the time to leave a review. It will help other find this book and it can help change a life in the same way that it changed yours. If you have constructive feedback, please also leave a review. It will help me better understand what you, the reader, need to make significant improvements in your life. I will take your feedback and use it to improve this book so that it can become more powerful and beneficial to all those who encounter it.

REMEMBER TO JOIN THE GROUP NOW!

If you have not joined the Mastermind Self Development group yet, now is your time! You will receive videos and articles from top authorities in self development as well as a special group only offers on new books and training programs. There will also be a monthly member only draw that gives you a chance to win any book from your Kindle wish list!

If you sign up through this link http://www.mastermindselfdevelopment.com/specialreport you will also get a special free report on the Wheel of Life. This report will give you a visual look at your current life and then take you through a series of exercises that will help you plan what your perfect life looks like. The workbook does not end there; we then take you through a process to help you plan how to achieve that perfect life. The process is very powerful and has the potential to change your life forever. Join the group now and start to change your life!
http://www.mastermindselfdevelopment.com/specialreport

You will also love these other great titles from Mastermind Self Development!

You will want to check out these other great titles Mastermind Self Development. All available in the Kindle store or you can just click on covers below.

http://viewbook.at/veganbook

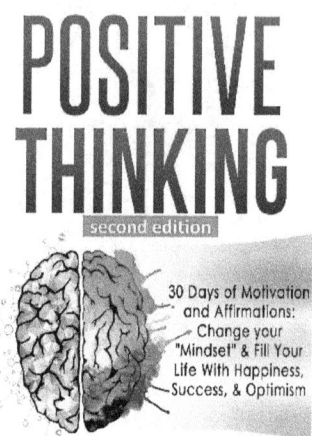

http://mybook.to/positivethink

You can also find these titles by searching them in the Kindle store on Amazon.

Learn Spanish:

A Fast and Easy Guide for Beginners to Learn Conversational Spanish

Table of Contents

Introduction

Chapter 1: Spanish - How does it work?

Chapter 2: Pronunciation

Chapter 3: Basic Conversation

Chapter 4: Pronouns Redux: Direct Object and Indirect Object

Conclusion

© Copyright 2017 by Mastermind Self Development All rights reserved.

The follow eBook is reproduced below with the goal of providing information that is as accurate and reliable as possible. Regardless, purchasing this eBook can be seen as consent to the fact that both the publisher and the author of this book are in no way experts on the topics discussed within and that any recommendations or suggestions that are made herein are for entertainment purposes only. Professionals should be consulted as needed prior to undertaking any of the action endorsed herein.

This declaration is deemed fair and valid by both the American Bar Association and the Committee of Publishers Association and is legally binding throughout the United States.

Furthermore, the transmission, duplication or reproduction of any of the following work including specific information will be considered an illegal act irrespective of if it is done electronically or in print. This extends to creating a secondary or tertiary copy of the work or a recorded copy and is only allowed with express written consent from the Publisher. All additional right reserved.

The information in the following pages is broadly considered to be a truthful and accurate account of facts and as such any inattention, use or misuse of the information in question by the reader will render any resulting actions solely under their purview. There are no scenarios in which the publisher or the original author of this work can be in any fashion deemed liable for any hardship or damages that may befall them after undertaking information described herein.

Additionally, the information in the following pages is intended only for informational purposes and should thus be thought of as universal. As befitting its nature, it is presented without assurance regarding its prolonged validity or interim quality. Trademarks that are mentioned are done without written consent and can in no way be considered an endorsement from the trademark holder.

Introduction

Congratulations on downloading Learn Spanish: A Fast and Easy Guide for Beginners to Learn Conversational Spanish and thank you for doing so.

The following chapters will discuss how you can start speaking Spanish fast. This book is based around a method that I've developed and curated alongside and based off of some of the most prolific language learners and educators of the modern age.

Why learn Spanish? Well, I'm sure that if you picked up this book, you already had a reason, but it's worth going a bit more into it anyway. You should learn Spanish because, simply put, it's a rich language.

Over the last several centuries, Spanish has been across multiple continents and forged connections between all of them. Spanish has persisted as a linguistic force since the Spanish empire began to cover the world over. The language spoken now isn't quite the same as the language spoken in the 15th century on the first voyage to the new world, but the similarities between that variety of Spanish and the modern day variety of Spanish sets you up for libraries worth of literature from all over the world in the Spanish language.

What's more is the sheer beauty of the fact that Spanish, since it's covered the world over, has taken in a number of influences from other languages. Through its journey starting as a mere dialectical splinter of Vulgar Latin (the version of Latin spoken by the general populace of the Roman Republic and the Roman Empire), Spanish has picked up plenty of influences from all kinds of different languages and cultures, most notably from Arabic during the Arab occupation of Spain from the 700s to around the thirteenth century, but also from the Goths, the Basques, the Native Americans, and the Celts.

So in other words, when you learn Spanish, you're setting yourself up to be involved in learning a whole wealth of cultural and historical information in what is a relatively passive manner. That sheer attachment to history is one of the most beautiful things about learning language in general.

However, there are a great number of reasons otherwise for which you might learn Spanish. The growth of the Latin American population and the dissemination of Latin American culture into the United States provides an excellent opportunity in two ways. Firstly, you will inevitably be a more attractive candidate for various careers from a perspective of qualifications. Your ability to speak Spanish will make you an asset in more ways than you can possibly fathom, and a huge number of companies will be lining up in order to get you to work with them, especially if you're specialized in another manner too. Secondly, you'll have opened the door to talking to a whole new set of people. No longer will you be relegated to speaking simply to people who know and understand English;

rather, you'll be able to speak to and with people from the culturally beautiful continents of South America and Central America and the wonderful Latin American people. It will also enable you to go to travel to Spain with ease and talk to numerous people who are native Spanish speakers and, more importantly, natives to the *region*, which will most certainly help you to understand the culture, customs, and realities of the place that you're in.

I've already mentioned how Spanish is a language with an absolutely colossal reach, and with that in mind, I feel as though it's necessary to make a certain stipulation. Just like the English spoken in the United States, the English spoken in Australia, and the English spoken in England are vastly different, likewise is the Spanish of Spain, the Spanish of Mexico, and the Spanish of, say, Argentina. They're different in manner of accent and dialect and some basic things, such as the usage of "vosotros" in Castilian Spanish (*Castellano*), or the Spanish of mainland Spain, where instead "ustedes" is used in Latin American Spanish. There's also the fact that certain dialects use the pronoun *vos*, which is generally never used otherwise and sounds rather booky and antiquated in the same way that using the pronoun *thou* sounds in English.

There are plenty of books on this subject on the market, thanks again for choosing this one! Every effort was made to ensure it is full of as much useful information as possible, please enjoy! I can guarantee that by the end of this book, you're going to feel comfortable speaking and reading Spanish.

Chapter 1: Spanish - how does it work?

In the United States, there's an institution called the *Foreign Service Institute*. What they do is train people, generally federal agents such as diplomats, in order to be prepared to go overseas in order to promote United States interests. They provide a huge number of courses in over seventy foreign languages and are one of the authorities on language learning in the United States.

The Foreign Service Institute has a list of languages cut into categories based upon how difficult they are for native English speakers to pick up and learn. Languages such as Arabic, Chinese, and Japanese rank among the hardest, being placed in category V: languages which are "exceptionally difficult for native English speakers."

Languages such as Danish, French, and indeed Spanish place, fortunately, in the simplest ranking: category I, which contains languages closely related to language.

A given language makes their way into this category in several ways. For example, they might share similar sentence structure and grammar to English. On top of that, they might share a lot of common vocabulary (many of the languages in category I developed alongside each other.)

What does this mean for you as a student learner of Spanish? Primarily, it means that you should have an easy enough time getting acquainted with the language and finding your way around it.

In fact, there are a laundry list of similarities between Spanish and English. Take this lightly, however. I've said it a million times before across multiple books: you shouldn't focus on the similarities. There are a few reasons for this.

The first major reason for not getting caught up on minor similarities is that eventually you're going to run into what the French call *faux amis* - "false friends." These are words which sound like they would mean one thing in English but mean a totally different thing in Spanish. Take, for example, the word "éxito." This is a Spanish word, and when an English speaker looks at it, they assume boldly that it means "exit", because, well, it looks like it means "exit". The Spanish word for "exit", though, is "salida" - the word "éxito" actually means "success"! Very, very different word.

There are a huge number more true cognates - words which mean exactly what it sounds like between Spanish and English - than false cognates. But that doesn't mean that it's not too easy to hear very common false cognates and think that they're a certain English word when they're not. This stems from two problems: first, it stems from the person making the bold assumption that English and Spanish must have something in common simply because a given word sounds similarly. This is nowhere *near* the truth, as it frankly shouldn't ever be. And secondly, it stems from a lack of looking at the word contextually and trying to truly figure out what it means given the other words in the sentence. The idea of "context" is your best friend when doing any sort of immersion based language learning, so learning to use it at its most appropriate and as often as you possibly can is wholly essential.

The second major reason for not getting caught up on minor similarities is that, frankly, every language has a lot more in common than things that set them apart. Perhaps not in the context of vocabulary - and there are also things among various languages which are particularly niche and neat, such as the Japanese and Korean languages' ideas of "topic markers" - but at the end of the day, languages are far more *similar* than they are different. After all, what is language, really? Language is simply a method of using our ability to speak in order to transmit and process information between one another. It's the apex of human cooperation. In that respect, every language is serving the same purpose: transmittance and processing of given tidbits of information. And all information has something in common: the rational devolution of a sentence into smaller pseudo-concepts. For example, different languages may place them differently, but every single language has a mechanism for denoting the bare linguistic essentials, like subjects (the thing around which the sentence is formed), actions (the things which the subject undertakes), objects (the thing which receives or acts as recipient of the action), as well as various modifiers in order to further and better describe things.

So to get stuck on the similarities between Spanish and English is absolutely absurd, because to point out the similarities is to say things such as "Spanish and English both have *objects*", "Spanish and English both have *pronouns*", and "Spanish and English both have some degree of Latin derivation due to their historical basis from mainland Europe." That's practically useless information in the grand context of language learning.

The things which actually matter in the context of language learning are found in the *differences*. The same basic mechanisms will persist, albeit manifested differently.

So what are the differences between English and Spanish? Well, despite the similarity of the two languages, they're numerous.

For one, Spanish has a very different system of pronunciation to English. It's far more regular but also a fair bit more nuanced in the specific sounds. With the espoused regularity of Spanish pronunciation comes a fair amount of adjustment from our English alphabet where a given letter can stand in for any number of different sounds. What this essentially means is that Spanish offers a far more rigid system of pronunciation which makes it easier to speak and learn, but it also means that you'll simultaneously have to undo some of the pronunciation consistencies that you've subconsciously learned while speaking English, which can be a lot easier said than done. Anyhow. we'll go more into the specific pronunciation of words in the second chapter.

Lesson one: Gendered nouns

Another way that Spanish differs is that it treats adverbs and adjectives far differently than English does. This might not sound terribly menacing at first, but it can definitely be difficult to keep up with early on in you're learning. The reason that it's so weird is because Spanish has something called *gendered nouns*. I'm introducing this concept to you early because it's the one which is bound to trip you up first and, as such, it deserves to be the first concept which you really work with.

Spanish applies genders to every single noun. For example, the word for *banana* is masculine (*plátano*), while the word for *table* is feminine (*mesa*).

So what does this mean? Does this mean that tables are meant for women and bananas are meant for men? That a woman eating a banana implies that she's doing something not "ladylike"? No, not at all.

The concept of gendered nouns is a purely grammatical concept and has nothing to do with any kind of innate masculinity or femininity of a noun. It's actually a concept which dates back to vulgar Latin, where there were three articles (we'll talk about those in a moment) known as *ille, illa,* and *illud*. Well, they were actually demonstrative adjectives, but that's another discussion entirely. These would be used by the common people in order to refer to specific instances of a noun, and which one you use would largely depend upon the ending sound of the word which came before it. This is a concept known as "vowel harmony". In other words, the concept of grammatical gender is wholly and entirely a solely linguistic concept and has more to do with the harmony of certain phrases than any sort of innate characteristics of the object deciding whether it is "male" or "female". There actually used to be another gender, the *neuter* gender, which was just a third grammatical category for nouns. This gender, however, was dropped with time.

Lesson two: Articles

Articles in Spanish act rather differently to those in English. They correspond specifically to the noun in question in terms of gender and plurality.

English doesn't do this so much. To compare this sort of difference, let's first analyze English's article system.

In English, there are two articles: *the* and either *a* or *an* depending on whether the next work begins with a vowel or a consonant sound. *The* is what's called a definite article, and *a/an* are what are called indefinite articles.

A *definite article* is an article which has a direct correspondence to a specifically stated object in space. For example, take the sentence "have you turned *the* television on today?" Because of the phrasing of this sentence, you can assume that they're referring to one very specific television which would either be denoted by context (perhaps you're all in the living room and the television won't turn on) or by a clause which specifically denotes which object is being referred to. ("Did you turn the television *in the living room* on today?")

An *indefinite article* is an article which lacks the specificity of the direct article. That is to say that the *indefinite article* refers to a non-specific instance of an object in space. If somebody were to ask you "have you turned *a* television on today?", you would think it was bizarre - principally because when would somebody ask that question? - but you would also likely say "yes" or "no" depending on whether or not you have indeed turned on *any* given television at some point in the day.

This distinction also exists in Spanish, but it's a bit more nuanced.

Spanish has four different *definite articles* which respond to the gender and plurality of an object. For these examples, I'm going to reuse the *banana* and *table* words.

The Spanish definite articles are as follows:

El - singular masculine definite

La - singular feminine definite

Los - plural masculine or mixed definite

Las - plural feminine definite

When I say the "masculine or mixed definite", I mean that if you have a group of people that are of either gender, or objects which are of either gender, then you should use "los". If every given object to which you're directly referring is feminine, then and only then should you use "las".

Spanish also has four different *indefinite articles*. The Spanish articles can broadly translate to either "a", "an", or "some" dependent upon the context.

The Spanish indefinite articles are as follows:

Un - singular masculine indefinite

Una - singular feminine indefinite

Unos- plural masculine or mixed indefinite

Unas - plural feminine indefinite

So how would I relate these to the two nouns I already know at this point? Simple. Let's run through a few basic exercises. Quick reminder that the term for *banana* is *el plátano* and the term for *table* is *la mesa*. Plurality in Spanish works by simply appending an *s*, just like it works in English.

1. Translate "the tables".
2. Translate "some bananas".

3. Translate "a table".
4. Translate "the bananas."

Your answers should have come out as follows:

1. *Las mesas*
2. *Unos plátanos*
3. *Una mesa*
4. *Los plátanos*

The reason that they come out like that is pretty plain. There's not a whole lot going on here, the main things to take away from this lesson is that nouns have specific genders in Spanish, as they do in other Romance languages and a quarter of languages in the world, actually.

There's one more problem we encounter here: the *uncountable nouns* issue. For example, you can eat three peaches, but you can't drink three waters. In the case of an uncountable noun - usually a liquid, but could be any variety of things - you're to not use an article at all.

Lesson three: Subject pronouns

So at the moment, what we're trying to do is form very basic Spanish sentences with a really cursory amount of knowledge that will create a baseline level of Spanish for you to work with going forward.

Sentences in any given language have three basic components, at the minimum: a *subject*, an *object*, and a *verb*. We've covered the basics of introducing objects to your Spanish by covering the bare essentials of nouns and noun gendering. However, in order to do a lot more with this lesson, we really have to critically analyze the whole concept of *subject pronouns* before we can really make our way onto verbs. Spanish verbs are far, *far* more complex than English ones (despite having relatively simpler conjugation rules than a large number of other concurrent Romance languages).

Subject pronouns form the very basis of the most basic sentences. If you don't know what a pronoun is, it is essentially the word which replaces the subject in a sentence.

We make extensive use of this in English, because we really like to talk in the first person. What I mean by this is that if somebody's name were John, and you were having a discussion with him, it would sound terribly awkward if he said "John is going to the store later. John is excited, because John is going to get the stuff to make curry." That simply doesn't work for the way that we structure sentences. We far prefer to *change* those words to the first-person subject pronoun in order to make it sound more accurate and give more context as to who is speaking. This makes fundamentally more sense from a linguistic perspective, too. When we say "I", there's no question about who is speaking - you're referring to yourself. So the distinction between the "I" and actually saying your name is totally unnecessary.

Spanish has these distinctions are well. Spanish actually has a few more of these distinctions than we do - I'll get to that in a second.

The Spanish pronouns are as follows:

Yo - I

Tú - You (singular, informal)

Usted - You (singular, formal)

Él - He/It (masculine)

Ella - She/It (feminine)

Nosotros - We

Ustedes - You (plural) (Latin America)

Vosotros - You (plural) (Spain)

Ellos - Male/masculine or mixed gender group

Ellas - Female/feminine group

Remember that we're working with explicitly Latin American Spanish in this book, and as such, we aren't going to really mess around with conjugating the *vosotros* pronoun. There are three key differences from English in this set-up of subject pronouns.

The first major difference is the separation of the *tú* and *usted* informal and formal pronouns. In English, no such distinction exists. In Middle English it did, as the distinction between *thou* and *you*; however, this has faded away with time as *you* has taken precedence. In case you're unfamiliar with informal and formal pronouns: you use the informal when you're speaking to somebody that you know well, such as a family member or friend, or somebody younger than you. You use the formal when you're speaking to somebody in a position of authority over you, or when you're meeting somebody for the first time.

The next major difference is that Spanish has an official verb for the second-person plural. This is another thing that we don't have in English. This entire idea is actually rather foreign to English. This place is filled by colloquial phrases. In the Southern United States, "y'all" fills the niche; in the Northeast, "youse"; in the Midwest, "you guys". There is not, however, a relatively standardized form, nor is there a singular word. (Even "y'all" is a contraction of the phrase "you all".)

The third major difference is that the Spanish don't have a specific word for "it". The reason for this is obvious if you think about it: they don't have a neuter pronoun or neuter gender *at all*. That concept is missing from Spanish completely in modernity. As such, since every item has either a feminine or masculine grammatical gender, it makes perfect sense to simply use the feminine and masculine pronouns in order to refer to it in a way.

The reason that we're spending a while on this topic is so that you're prepared for the next topic, which will be a lot heavier: *verb conjugation*. But for the concept of verb conjugation, you have to have a subject in the first place to conjugate for.

Without further ado, let's move to the next lesson, which no doubt is of astronomical importance.

Lesson four: Basic verb conjugation (-er verbs)

So what is verb conjugation? In English, we have a very simplified form. Verb conjugation is simply the changing of the ending of a given verb, or action word, depending upon the person who's performing it. A lot of the verb conjugation in English has fallen away with time. In its place is only a very simple remnant.

Let's take the verb "*to run*" (this form being called the "infinitive") and conjugate it in the present tense.

I run

You run

He/she/it run**s**

We run

They run

The only form of verb conjugation which occurs in the present tense is the adding of the *-s* to the third person singular form.

This is a very different story from Spanish. Spanish is an absolutely beautiful and expressive language. Along with this comes a huge amount of caveats concerning writing and speaking, though.

The heavy conjugation system, however, does have some bright sides. The fact that verbs end differently depending upon who is speaking means that generally, the subject pronoun can (and will) be dropped altogether. This means that sentences are, of course, far more expressive and clear than they often would be otherwise, while also being more economical.

So how do you conjugate a basic present tense verb in Spanish?

Let's look at this using the verb *comer*, meaning *to eat*.

Comer - *to speak*

Conjugation	Meaning	Pronunciation
Yo com*o*.	I eat.	yoh coh-moh
Tú com*es*.	You eat.	too coh-mehs
Él/ella/usted com*e*.	He/she/you eat.	el/ey-yah/oos-ted coh-meh
Nosotros com*emos*.	We eat.	noh-soh-tros coh-meh-mos
Ellos/Ellas/Ustedes com*en*.	They/they/you all eat.	ey-yohs/ey-yahs/oos-ted-ehs coh-mehn

This gives you a very simple summary of how to conjugate a regular *-er* verb in Spanish. There are two other verb forms, which we'll get to momentarily, as well as a slew of irregular verbs, with what are in fact the most common verbs in the language being irregular. We'll also get to those momentarily.

You'll notice in the conjugation table that depending upon who is speaking, the end of the word would change. This is the bare essence of verb conjugation: changing the word in accordance with who is speaking.

There are a whole host of regular -er verbs that you'll find useful. I'm going to give you the conjugation tables for two more, before giving you a bunch of them to practice with.

Vender - *to sell*

Conjugation	Meaning	Pronunciation
Yo vend*o*.	I sell.	yoh vehn-doh
Tú vend*es*.	You sell.	too vehn-dehs
Él/ella/usted vend*e*.	He/she/you sell.	el/ey-yah/oos-ted vehn-deh
Nosotros vend*emos*.	We sell.	noh-soh-tros vehn-deh-mos
Ellos/Ellas/Ustedes vend*en*.	They/they/you all sell.	ey-yohs/ey-yahs/oos-ted-ehs vehn-dehn

Comprender - *to understand*

Conjugation	Meaning	Pronunciation
Yo comprend*o*.	I understand.	yoh cohm-prehn-doh
Tú comprend*es*.	You understand.	too cohm-prehn-dehs
Él/ella/usted comprend*e*.	He/she/you understand.	el/ey-yah/oos-ted cohm-prehn-dehs
Nosotros comprend*emos*.	We understand.	noh-soh-tros cohm-prehn-mos
Ellos/Ellas/Ustedes comprend*en*.	They/they/you all eat.	ey-yohs/ey-yahs/oos-ted-ehs coh-mehn

By now, you should see a very tangible pattern among these. With that in mind, I'm going to give you a few more super common -*er* verbs before we move on to conjugating -*ar* and -*ir* verbs.

Practice verbs:

- aprender: *to learn*
- beber: *to drink*
- poseer: *to possess* or *to own*
- responder: *to respond* or *to answer*
- ofender: *to offend*
- promete: *to promise*
- someter: *to submit*

Lesson five: Regular verb conjugation with -ar and -ir verbs

With the very basics of verb conjugation out of the way, we can now move onto the other verb forms. As I said, Spanish verb forms tend to take three types: -*er*, -*ar*, or -*ir*. Sadly, a lot of the most common verbs are irregular and don't follow traditional conjugation, but that's just what happens when you have a lot of people speaking a language over a lot of space and saying these words constantly: uniformity falls away to slang as the natural process of linguistic evolution is exacerbated by constant usage. But with that said, the vast wealth of Spanish verbs are indeed regular, they just don't happen to be quite as common. Anyway, we'll get to regular verbs in the next lesson.

The first thing that we're going to cover here is the concept of conjugating -*ar* verbs. We're going to start this process out with the verb *hablar*, meaning "to speak".

Hablar - *to speak*

Conjugation	Meaning	Pronunciation
Yo habl*o*.	I speak.	yoh ah-bloh
Tú habl*as*.	You speak.	too ah-blahs
Él/ella/usted habl*a*.	He/she/you speak.	el/ey-yah/oos-ted ah-blah
Nosotros habl*amos*.	We speak.	noh-soh-tros ah-blah-mos
Ellos/Ellas/Ustedes habl*an*.	They/they/you all speak.	ey-yohs/ey-yahs/oos-ted-ehs ah-blahn

You'll notice that a lot of these conjugations are superbly similar to the same conjugations for *-er* verbs, and you'd be right to notice that. The only major noticeable difference between the two is that these verbs, of course, take an *a* in place of the *e*.

-ir verbs act similarly and, in fact, aren't that different either. In fact, their conjugation is exactly the same as *-er* verbs, except for the "Nosotros" form. Observe what I mean as we conjugate the verb *discutir*, meaning "to discuss".

Discutir - *to discuss*

Conjugation	Meaning	Pronunciation
Yo discut*o*.	I discuss.	yoh dees-cooh-toh
Tú discut*es*.	You discuss.	too dees-cooh-tehs
Él/ella/usted discut*e*.	He/she/you discuss.	el/ey-yah/oos-ted dees-cooh-teh
Nosotros discut*imos*.	We discuss.	noh-soh-tros dees-cooh-tee-mos
Ellos/Ellas/Ustedes discut*en*.	They/they/you all discuss.	ey-yohs/ey-yahs/oos-ted-ehs dees-coo-tehn

Indeed, you'll see that there's little to no difference in the conjugation of these *-ir* verbs in the present tense than conjugating *-er* verbs in the present tense aside from the *nosotros* form.

By now, you've conjugated verbs in all forms, so the only thing you can do now is practice. That's how one genuinely and truly picks up skill in verb conjugation. At first, it will be ugly and very much not fun, but after a little practice, you'll be able to do it with absolute ease.

Here are some verbs with which you can practice your conjugating.

-ar verbs:

- caminar: *to walk*
- esperar: *to hope*
- comprar: *to buy*
- ayudar: *to help*
- viajar: *to travel*
- trabajar: *to work*

-ir verbs:

- vivir: *to live*
- debatir: *to debate*
- describir: *to describe*
- unir: *to unite*
- escribir: *to write*
- reunir: *to meet*

Of course there's an endless wealth of Spanish verbs that you can work with, and a little personal research certainly wouldn't be out of the question if you were so inclined. You know how to conjugate these verbs now, and it's on your pto practice it.

Lesson six: Irregular verbs, part one

The hardest part of coming to a new Romance language is frankly not learning conjugation. I've studied quite a few and conjugation comes relatively easy at this point. After all, it's a very finite system with little that ever really changes about it. No, the hardest part is totally and completely getting used to each language's irregular verbs and the numerous idiomatic ways in which they use their irregular verbs.

Given that this is a Spanish book, I won't give you the details all about, say, French or Italian's conjugation system. However, with the fact that it's a Spanish book established, we do need to move on to talking about how to actually conjugate and use these verbs.

The first one that we really need to cover is **ser**, which translates to "to be". It's actually one of two state of being verbs that Spanish has, and between it and the other verb *estar*, the general bases of the verb "to be" as it's used in English are covered.

Of course, the downside of having two verbs for something we represent with one in English is that, naturally, it's more efficient and expressive, but this also comes with the fact that for native English speakers it can be a terribly big adjustment to make linguistically. If you aren't used to representing these sort of ideas using two distinct verbs, then it's going to be a very odd thing for you to start to do so.

So with that said, when does one actually venture out and try to use *ser*? There are a few situations which call for *ser* specifically. The first time in which you'd use *ser* is in situations which specifically refer to things which are essential to you or somebody else's identity. These include things such as any physical description, your personality and your sense of character, the country that you're from, the race that you are, the gender that you are, what you do for a living, and what any given thing in general is made of.

Another time that you'd use *ser* is to donate any given thing which occurs or takes place at a point in time, such as dates, seasons, events, and time in general.

So how do we conjugate *ser*? Since *ser* is irregular, it'd most likely be easy for you starting out to simply try to remember the following conjugation table, which will come naturally anyhow with practice:

Ser - *to be*

Conjugation	Meaning	Pronunciation
Yo *soy*.	I am.	yoh soy
Tú *eres*.	You are.	too eh-res
Él/ella/usted *es*.	He/she/you are.	el/ey-yah/oos-ted es
Nosotros *somos*.	We are.	noh-soh-tros soh-mos
Ellos/Ellas/Ustedes *son*.	They/they/you are.	ey-yohs/ey-yahs/oos-ted-ehs sohn

So if you wanted to say, for example, "I'm from the United States", that's an intrinsic quality and description of you, so you would use *ser* here. "I'm from the United States" is a nifty sentence because it can actually translate quite directly from English into Spanish.

Yo *soy* de <u>los Estados Unidos</u>.*

I *am* from <u>the United States</u>.

* bear in mind that in conventional spoken Spanish, the "yo" would be dropped since the person who is speaking is implied directly through the verb conjugation.

So with all of that noted, when would we use the other word for *to be*, "estar"? Well, there are a few different cases in which you would use *estar*. It really depends. A good way to remember the usage of *estar* is the following rhyme often taught in high schools: "how you feel and where you are, that is when you use *estar*."

That rhyme, though simple, is not terribly far off base at all. The first usage of *estar* is, indeed, where you are. *Estar*'s principle usage is "emotional and physical states of being". These are temporary things like moods or appearances. This can make quite a massive difference. If you were to say:

Soy enojado.

Wherein *enojado* means "angry", you'd be essential telling the world that you're a very angry person in general. You'd be saying that anger is an essential personality description of you, a permanent fixture of description for you. This is fine if you're, for example, an angsty teenager who is mad at the world or popular multi-million selling rap artist Eminem, but otherwise, you most likely should use *estar*. Using *estar* here makes a world of difference. When used with emotion or states of being, *estar* can often also stand in for the word "feel" in English: *estar enojado* means "to be feeling angry", which removes the existential burden of being an angry person in general off of your back.

Estar is also the verb that you're supposed to use in order to indicate your location at a given time. Use *estar* in order to say that you're in either this place or that. You can use *estar* in order to denote the location of both people and of things.

So into the belly of the beast: how do we conjugate *estar*? Like so:

Estar - *to be (states of being)*

Conjugation	Meaning	Pronunciation
Yo *estoy*.	I am/feel.	yoh es-toy
Tú *estás*.	You are/feel.	too es-tahs
Él/ella/usted *está*.	He/she/you are/feel.	el/ey-yah/oos-ted es-tah
Nosotros *estamos*.	We are/feel.	noh-soh-tros es-tah-mos
Ellos/Ellas/Ustedes *están*.	They/they/you all are/feel.	ey-yohs/ey-yahs/oos-ted-ehs es-tahn

The distinction between *soy* and *estar* isn't terribly difficult to ascertain once you've got a grasp on it, but it will take two things in order for you to understand nuances like this fully: the first is *practice*. In order to understand how to use these verbs correctly - and indeed, a great number of Spanish words and idioms and phrases in general - you're going to have to practice using them correct. The second is *immersion*. Without proper immersion, you're well doomed. Luckily, modern society makes it very easy to simulate immersion in several different ways, such as watching television shows in other languages or signing up to talk to people who speak another language via services such as italki. Immersion is what allows you to hear the various uses of different phrases and understand how certain ideas and words are used in the context of another language.

Lesson seven: Tenses, part one

There's one more important distinction and usage of *estar* that we haven't really covered yet. Aside from its obvious appearance in Spanish idioms, there's a very important tense that we need to talk about: the present progressive.

Depending on your experiences with other languages, you may or may not be familiar with the common usage of the present progressive. Some languages don't have a present progressive tense in common use, such as French and Danish. English, however, takes great advantage of the present progressive tense.

What the present progressive tense does is indicate an action which is in the process of occurring. For example, if you were studying French, you might run into the sentence "Je chante". This can carry a meaning of either "I sing" in a general sense, or it can carry the meaning of "I am *currently* singing." French has this in a colloquial sense (the phrase "être en train de *verb*" can indicate an ongoing process) but in literature and more formal usage, there is no real equivalent for the present progressive - the simple present tense is used.

In Spanish and English, however, we make this distinction. For example, the phrase "I eat meat" would generally mean that somebody eats meat as a general part of their diet, but by inclusion of the verb "to be" and morphing "eat" into its gerund (the noun form of a verb), we can form the sentence "I *am* eat*ing* meat." which indicates that as we speak, we are eating meat.

Spanish has a very similar system. They too use *estar*, meaning of course "to be", in order to form the present progressive. as well as forming a present participle much like we form gerunds.

The way that the present participle is formed in Spanish is by looking at what kind of verb it is. If it's an *-er* or *-ir* verb, you just drop the ending and replace it with *-iendo*. This means that a verb like *someter*, which we discovered earlier means "to submit", would take on the form *somiendo*. For *-ar* verbs, what you would do is drop the *-ar* ending and replace it with *-ando*. So the verb *trabajar*, again meaning "to work", would become *trabajando*.

So depending upon who is speaking, one would simply conjugate *estar* to the correct form and then stick the present participle after it.

Let's practice! Translate the following:

1) I am working. (trabajar)
2) She is learning. (aprender)
3) You are writing. (escribir)

Your responses should have been as follows:

1) *Estoy trabajando.*
2) *Está aprendiendo.*
3) *Estás escribiendo.*

Are you seeing how this works, a tad? It's a relatively simple tense to form but it can be bizarre.

When you try to form present participles, remember also that not all verbs are created equal. Some, because they have endings which would make appending *-iendo* or *-ando* sound strange, don't have regular endings in the present participle. Be wary of this and, as always, be sure to research constantly as you learn. There's little more important than testing your limits, but being sure that the way you're testing them is correct is definitely up there.

Lesson eight: Working with "haber"

There are quite a few irregular verbs in Spanish. Somewhere close to around 34 percent. And the most common verbs are more likely to be irregular, too, go figure. For example, of the fifteen most common verbs in Spanish, *thirteen out of fifteen* can be described as irregular. It's absolutely absurd.

What this means for you as a language learner is that you are going to have to dedicate yourself to not only knowing normal regular verb conjugations but to knowing how to conjugate the irregular verbs, as well. Some of them have fall into patterns which are easily recognized, such as *hacer* and *decir* or *tener* and *poner*. Others, not so much.

Because of all of this, it can be rather difficult to really know where to start. The answer is that there is not quite a "right" place to start - it's just something that you're going to have to learn as you go on and attempt to use the words or hear the words used.

However, I do think that it's certainly sensible to start with the most *common* irregular verbs first, because you're far more likely to use them on a sentence to sentence basis. So with that said, let's start working a bit more with these irregular verbs and practicing them so that they get mentally tucked away for later use whenever you may need them once more.

The only other major irregular verb that we're going to work with in the context of this book is *haber*. This verb means roughly "to have" (though not in the sense of possessing something - for that purpose, you would use *poseder* instead). *Haber* means "to have" in the sense of the past, which we'll get to in a bit when we discuss more tenses.

Aside from this case (usage as an auxiliary verb), *haber* primarily is used in two other contexts. We'll discuss that after conjugating. Here's how you'd conjugate *haber*.

Haber - *to have*

Conjugation	Meaning	Pronunciation
Yo he.	I have.	yoh eh
Tú has.	You have.	too ahs
Él/ella/usted ha *or* hay.	He/she/you have.	el/ey-yah/oos-ted ah *or* eye
Nosotros hemos.	We have.	noh-soh-tros eh-mos
Ellos/Ellas/Ustedes han *or* hay.	They/they/you all have.	ey-yohs/ey-yahs/oos-ted-ehs ahn *or* eye

So, *haber* when not used to construct the perfect tense usually is used in one of two manners.

Firstly, it may be used in order to say "there is". It's not a direct translation, but if you think about it, it doesn't need to be. "There is" is a nonsensical impersonal phrase. All that it directly implies is the fact that something *is*, in the something *exists*. So *hay* is as much an equivalent phrase in Spanish as *il y a* is in French.

This is simple enough. Let's take that word for banana again, *plátano*. If we wanted to say there is a banana on the table. We'd do this like so:

There's a banana on the table.

Hay uno plátano en la mesa.

It works similarly for doubled objects where we'd otherwise use "There are" as opposed to "There is" in English.

There are three bananas on the table.

Hay tres plátanos en la mesa.

We needed to discuss the usage and implementation of *haber* because that brings us into our next lesson.

Lesson nine: A few more tenses...

I don't think that it would be particularly worthwhile in the scope of a beginner's book intended for people absolutely new to Spanish and perhaps even language learning in general for me to go through every single tense that you might use. My entire goal with this book at large is to get you to understand the underlying grammatical concepts so that you might actually be able to build on them through proper experimentation as well as through constantly trying out new things with the language.

However, there are two more tenses we're going to cover, both of them in the past tense. The reason we're not covering future tense is that for near future verbs, Spanish generally just uses the present tense anyhow, often alongside a time marker. The other Spanish future tense is meant for dates and events which are farther off, and in my opinion as somebody who writes about and works with languages, I don't think that's a particularly paramount subject for new learnings and I don't realistically see time spent on that tense to be worthwhile as a beginner.

What I will talk about however, is the *preterite* and the *perfect tense*.

The preterite is the tense which is used for events which are over and done with; things which happened once already and weren't continuous. This is the one that you need to focus on, and for a very simple reason: you very well may start off a conversation with the fact that you don't speak Spanish particularly well. And if you *were* to do that, you likely wouldn't even need the perfect tense at all. It's not likely or common for introductory Spanish speakers to feel the need to express themselves in the past tense in exclusive or esoteric ways.

If you need to form the preterite with an *-ar* verb, all you have to do is drop the -ar and append the following endings: -é, -aste, -ó, -amos, and -aron.

Here is the *-ar* preterite conjugated for the verb *enviar*.

Enviar - *to send (preterite)*

Conjugation	Meaning	Pronunciation
Yo *envié*.	I sent.	yoh ehn-vee-ey
Tú *enviaste*.	You sent.	too ehn-vee-ahs-tay
Él/ella/usted *envió*.	He/she/you sent.	el/ey-yah/oos-ted ehn-vee-oh
Nosotros *enviamos*.	We sent.	noh-soh-tros enviamos
Ellos/Ellas/Ustedes *enviaron*.	They/they/you all sent.	ey-yohs/ey-yahs/oos-ted-ehs ehn-vee-ah-rohn

Likewise, to form it for an *-er* or *-ir* verb, you just drop the ending and tack on either *-í, -iste, -ió, -imos,* or *-ieron*. Let's try this out really quickly by using the verb *vivir*.

Vivir - *to live (preterite)*

Conjugation	Meaning	Pronunciation
Yo *viví*.	I lived.	yoh vee-vee
Tú *viviste*.	You lived.	too vee-vees-tey.
Él/ella/usted *vivió*.	He/she/you lived.	el/ey-yah/oos-ted vee-vee-oh
Nosotros *vivimos*.	We lived.	noh-soh-tros vee-vee-mohs
Ellos/Ellas/Ustedes *vivieron*.	They/they/you all lived.	ey-yohs/ey-yahs/oos-ted-ehs vee-vee-ehr-ohn

The present perfect tense is very easy. All that you need is the verb *haber* and the verb you'd like to form into the present perfect.

The present perfect carries the same weight as saying something like "I have cooked" or "She has laughed" in English. It's not always a 1 to 1 correlation, but there are a lot of times where the situational usage will certainly match up. And what's more is that forming past participles is absurdly easy in Spanish for regular verbs. All that you do is drop the *-ar*, *-er*, or *-ir* ending and replace it, either with *-ado* for *-ar* verbs or *-ido* for *-ir* or *-er* verbs.

So if we were to take the verb *vivir* again, we could say "I have lived" in the present perfect tense like so:

(Yo) he vivido.

It's a really simple lesson to take home, but it's an important tense to understand nonetheless.

Lesson ten: one last thing...

In case you didn't know, you obviously can negate things in Spanish. You do so by simply adding *no* before the verb:

Como carne.

No como carne.

The first sentence means "I eat meat", and the second means "I don't eat meat". It's a simple lesson, but infinitely important nonetheless.

Chapter 2: Pronunciation

I'm going to be straightforward as I say this: as a Spanish learner, you have it easy. Spanish has ridiculously easy pronunciation compared to other languages. It makes up for it with difficulty in other areas and a bizarre amount of esotericism compared to other major Romance languages (largely due to Arab influence). However, Spanish pronunciation is simple and predictable. You're hardly going to have a problem with any of it going forward.

The first thing that we need to talk about is the basic vowel sounds. Coming from English, it's really easy to pronounce things like you would in English, especially if it resembles an English word that you know. However, you can't do this. Spanish vowels are absolutely finite in their pronunciation and not saying them correctly is the fast track to sounding like an absolutely inexperienced Spanish speaker.

Here are the vowel sounds for Spanish, alongside how they're pronounced.

a will sound much like the first O in *O*ctober.
e will sound like the *ay* in the word *bay* if the syllable ends in a vowel. If it ends in a consonant, then it will sound like the *e* in *net*.
i will sound like the *ee* in *tree*.
o will sound like the *o* in *rope* if the syllable ends in a vowel. If it ends in a consonant, it will sound like *o* in the word *hot*.
u will sound like the *oo* in *school*, unless it's in any of the following letter groups: gue, gui, qu. In these cases, it will be silent.
y will sound like the Spanish *i* when it is used as a vowel.

And naturally, Spanish has diphthongs as well. Diphthongs are the resultant sound of two vowels being put together. Generally, in Spanish at least, they're just the end result of the vowels being put together, and you can guess their sound just by putting the two appropriate vowel sounds together rather fast. Here are some common diphthongs regardless, and some familiar sounds you can associate with them:

ai will sound like the *i* in *bride*; **ay** will as well.
au will sound like the *ou* in *sound*.
ei will sound like the *ay* in *gray*; **ey** will as well.
eu will sound like the *ay-you* in *today-you*.
oi will sound like the *oy* in *coy*; **oy** will as well.
u before *any* vowel will sound like a *w*.
i before most vowels will sound like a *y*; **y** will as well.

Now it's time to move onto the consonant sounds. The consonant sounds will in certain places be very familiar, and if so, I'm not going to really bother expounding upon them. However, some are quite different, and so I'll go into detail on those.

B, if at the beginning of a word or when after a consonant, will sound like the English *b*. However, otherwise, it will sound like a mixture between an English *b* and an English *v*. **V** follows the same exact rules.

C, when it's before either a consonant or the vowels *a, u,* or *o*, will have a hard C sound like in "construction". Before the vowels *e* or *i*, however, the **C** will sound like an English *s*.

Ch always sounds the same: like the *ch* in *champion*. The reason I list this as it's own letter is twofold: firstly, English has both a *ch* and an *sh* sound reserved for the *ch* grouping. In Spanish, this isn't the case. However, there's also the fact that throughout history, the *ch* in Spanish has been treated as its own letter, before D but after C. Many older Spanish dictionaries and Spanish-English dictionaries will have the *Ch* words as their own category.

D will always sound like the English *d*, unless it's between vowels or following the letter *l* or the letter *n*, in either case it will be pronounced like the *th* in *that*.

F sounds like the English *f*.

G sounds like an English *h* but with more power, if before an *e* or an *i*; if it's before anything else, it sounds like the *g* in *gather*.

H is silent.

J sounds like an English *h* but with more power, and is silent whenever it is the last letter in a word.

K sounds like an English *k*.

L sounds like an English *l*.

Ll sounds like an English *y*, though it in some dialects has a slight *sh* sound to it. Pay attention to how the people around you pronounce it and mimic it, but use the *y* sound firstly.

M sounds like an English *m*.

N sounds like an English *n* in every instance except for when it precedes the letter *v*. In this case, it will sound like an English *m*.

Ñ sounds like an *ny* sound, as in *onion* or *bunion*.

P sounds like an English *p*.

Q is *always* followed by *u*, and the pair will *always* sound like an English *k*.

R is performed by way of an alveolar flap in the middle of a word, meaning a very soft touching of the tongue to the roof of the mouth. At the beginning of a given word or when it's following either the letter *l*, the letter *n*, or the letter *s*, it will have a powerful trill. At the end of a word, it has next to no trill, but still a small amount.

Rr indicates a very strong trill.

S will sound like an English *s* unless it's preceding either *b*, *d*, *g*, *l*, *m*, or *n*, in which case it will sound like an English *z*.

T will sound like an English *t*.

W will nearly always have a *v* sound. There are various linguistic reasons for this phenomenon, but I'm not going to go into them right here.

X sounds like an English *x* is between vowels, but before a given consonant it will sound like an English *s*. This is presuming the word isn't of Native or Aboriginal influence. If so, then it will sound like an *h*. (*Mexico* would sound like *Mey-hee-coh*, and *Texas* would sound like *Tey-hahs*.)

Y sounds like an English *y*.

Z generally just sounds like an English *z*.

As you can see, for the most part, Spanish pronunciation is generally very uniform. When there is a variation, change, or exception, it's likewise generally very easy to understand within the context of the language.

It's also worth noting the role of accent marks in Spanish. In the Spanish language, accent marks indicate *syllable stress* or serve to differentiate one word's spelling from another. This can be of grave importance, as some words without proper accents being written will take on totally different meanings which may at times even be personally embarrassing.

If you see an accent mark while reading Spanish, then it always means that you need to be certain that the syllable with the accent mark is getting quite a bit of stress and is enunciated *loudly* and *clearly*.

Chapter 3: Basic Conversation

I'd be doing you a major disservice if I didn't teach you the very basics of Spanish conversation. The reason I've held off to this point is because a lot of language courses will start off by giving you the basic phrases of a language. That's great for letting you say hello and goodbye to people, but when it comes to building statements with any sort of actual meat to them, it's an uphill battle because you don't actually know anything about the language yet.

For example, before you even picked up this book, you most likely at least knew the word *hola* from having heard it in any number of North American sources involving Spanish speakers. But how much does that matter for having genuine discussion with Spanish speakers? Does that knowledge of *hola* allow you in any capacity to walk up to a Spanish stranger and do anything but say "hello" to them?

The answer, of course, is no. That's an utterly ridiculous notion in most every possible conceivable way. That is thus the very reason that I've held off going over all of this up until now: it simply wasn't necessary and would get in the way of actually *understanding* Spanish in any sort of meaningful manner.

But now that you understand the pronunciation and a lot of basic verbiage, I feel as though we're at a reasonable point where I can give you introductions to conversation without making myself feel like I'm making the language seem like it's anything but what it is: a language, with a thriving set of verb conjugations and unique articles and all of these awesome features that extend far, far beyond "holá".

Anyhow, for the sake of this chapter, we're going to work through a number of phrases one at a time with a brief explanation of everything that we're doing.

The first thing that you do in any given conversation is *initiate* it. Well, this isn't necessarily always true - some people are very pragmatic and get right to the point. But for most people, saying salutations is just a normal part of any given conversation, or perhaps things which aren't even really conversation. Perhaps you're passing by somebody you know in the school or workplace and want to acknowledge them. That's another situation in which you'd find knowing salutations to be a great advantage.

Spanish has a great many salutations and the one that you use depends upon a number of variables, of course.

There's, of course, the general use *hola* (oh-la). This just means "hello" in English. The etymology of the word "hola" is deeply interesting, but it's of course beyond the scope of this book.

Anyhow, there are also the greetings which have to do with the time of day. There is *buenos días (bwey-nohs di-ahs)*. This means literally "good morning" and is one of the more common Spanish greetings aside from *hola*. There also is *buenas tardes (bwey-nahs tar-dehs)*, which means *good evening*. This isn't used as often as a conventional salutation, though it certainly can be used as one with no problem. The last one in this category is *buenas noches (bwey-nahs no-chess)*. This means literally "good night" and its usage is unwavering; you will almost never ever use this as a salutation. You generally will only use this as a goodbye to somebody for the night is you know that you won't be seeing them again that night.

Lastly, there is *muy buenos. (moy bwey-nohs)*. This is a very general greeting as compared to other ones such as *buenos días* and *hola*. You can use this greeting at pretty much any time of day without anybody batting an eye.

So after all of that, we're now officially in the conversation, engaging in the nigh professional art of small talk. These small talk sessions generally almost always start by asking somebody how they are or how they're doing. There are a ton of ways to ask this sort of question in Spanish.

Firstly, there are the more formal and boring routes to be taken. To simply ask "How are you?", you first need to think about who you're talking to. Are you speaking to somebody your age? Younger? Older? Have you met them before? Then you need to pick either the informal or the formal way to ask based upon your evaluations. The informal way to ask is to simply "*¿Cómo estas?*" (co-moh es-tahs), meaning in a literal sense "how are you?". The formal way is just the usted inversion of the prior question: *¿Cómo está usted? (co-moh es-ta oos-ted)*. This means the same thing as before, but this version is of course to be reserved for meeting new people or for talking to people who are in a position of superiority.

On top of that, there are more casual ways to ask. You could say "how's it going?": *¿Cómo te va?* (co-moh teh va)

Simply asking "what's up?" is certainly not out of the question: *¿Qué tal?* (kay tall)

Neither would be asking something along the lines of "what's happening?"- *¿Qué pasa?* (kay pah-sah) - or "How have you been?": *¿Cómo has ido?* (co-moh ahs ee-do)

All in all, there are a ton of ways to ask somebody exactly how they're doing in Spanish. There are likewise a huge number of ways in which you could respond to this very question. Note that being in a foreign country or situation means that the culture is inevitably different; in America and England, when we ask "how are you?", we do so as a courtesy and generally not in the seeking of a very well-thought out response or any sort of genuine emotional discourse. Certain other countries aren't like this, and if you ask how they are, they'll tell you how they are.

But for all intents and purposes, you may or may not give a very deep response. Should you choose to go with a more "standard" response, there are a number of different ways in which you could phrase it.

You could start with the quintessential *bien, gracias* (byen, grah-see-as) which means simply "well/fine, thank you." You could also opt for "very well" by saying *muy bien* (moy byen). You could insert a certain amount of nihilistic apathy into your conversation by saying *Como siempre* which technically means "like always" but carries the weight more like "I am as I always seem to be." If you're not feeling well, you can say that you're sick by saying either *estoy enfermo* or *estoy enferma* depending upon your gender, men saying the first and women saying the second. And if you're not doing too well, you could say *más o menos* (moss oh men-ohs) meaning "so-so", or you could say *mal* which translates to simply "badly" or "poorly".

Then, there are multiple different ways in which you could say goodbye. There are a few generally used ones, and a few which are geared towards more special purposes.

The two general purpose ones that you need to know are *adiós* and *chao*. Both are common enough that I'm not going to tell you how to pronounce them. If you're on the up, you very well may notice a parallel between Spanish and neighboring Romance language Italian here, where *ciao* is used as a form of goodbye. Both of these are acceptable ways to say goodbye.

If you'll be seeing the person soon, you could tell them *Hasta pronto (ahs-tah pronto)*. But when I say *soon*, I mean **soon**. This is one place where the common conception of "soon" as used in the U.S. or Britain generally doesn't cut it in other timetables.

If you're just going to see them at a later point in time, you could say *Hasta luego* (*ahs-tah lwey-go*). This could imply a lack of certainty about when you'll meet again, however. It, as many things do, ultimately depends upon the context in which it's used.

The last one we're going to talk about here is *Hasta la vista* (*ahs-tah lah vees-tah*, but honestly, who doesn't know how to pronounce this one thanks to Hollywood?). This phrase means essentially "Until next time" or "untill we meet again". This one too can communicate a lack of certainty dependent upon the context.

On top of all of that, there are some essential phrases that you have absolutely got to know in order to ask for help in Spanish, or otherwise get around.

Firstly, there are two forms of "excuse me" you need to know. The first, *perdón*, means "excuse me" in the sense of "excuse me, could I ask you about something?"

The other form of excuse me, *con permiso*, has a meaning more along the lines of "Please excuse me", when you're needing somebody to move out of your way.

You also need to know how to say thank you and sorry. In fact, more people need to know how to do this in their *native* language. The way that you say "thank you" in Spanish is straightforward: *Gracias*. Nearly everybody knows that term. And the way you say sorry is additionally simple: *Lo siento* (*lo syen-toh*).

It's most certainly also worth you learning how to say *please* in Spanish because you invariably are going to need to at some point. You do so by saying *por favor. (pour fah-vor)*

And lastly, at some point, eventually you're going to have to ask for help in some way, shape, or form. The way to do this is by saying *necesito ayuda* (*ney-cess-ee-toh ah-you-dah*). This means literally "I need help" or "I need aid". You'll also notice that this very simple phrase is built off of the verb *necesitar*, conjugated for the first person as worked with in chapter one.

There's a lot of things you'll need to learn before you're ready for the streets, but hopefully now, you've got a solid enough foundation you can at least be courteous.

Chapter 4: Pronouns Redux: Direct Object and Indirect Object

We spoke earlier in the book about the manifold uses of *subject pronouns* and how they're used in English in order to enrich our sentences and make them less monotonous or unwieldy, and how they're ditched almost entirely in Spanish after conjugating the verb due to their very verbose conjugation system.

It'd be a mortal sin for me to actually finish up this book and somehow leave out the idea of more advanced pronouns. You're going to inevitably end up needing to use these, and likely quite often. The manner by which we naturally speak English is absolutely littered with these things. They're peppered throughout essentially every sentence that we speak. The same manner of speaking applies to Spanish as well. Nobody on earth likes redundancy, and not having some kind of pronouns system in place not only endorses but *enforces* redundancy.

The first form of pronouns that we're going to focus on at this point in time are the *direct object pronouns*. Direct object pronouns are pronouns which stand in for the direct object of the sentence. In case you're unclear what a direct object is, it is the thing which takes the brunt of a verb or an action as indicated by the structure, context, and intention of the sentence.

I actually feel like before we jump into the *mechanics* of direct object pronouns, I should make the distinction between direct objects and indirect objects and why the distinction even really matters.

Direct objects are, as I said, objects which go along with the verb, whereas indirect objects are not. They are *affected* by the verb and the direct object, but they are in no way attached to them. The way that I like to say it is this: the sentiment of the sentence can completely and wholly exist even without the inclusion of the indirect object. It may be significantly vaguer, but the resultant thought is still a complete syntactically and grammatically correct sentence.

Take the following sentence for example:

I sent the card to her.

If we were to break this sentence down into its essential components, it would look as follows:

I - subject; indicates the person or thing which is actively undergoing the verb.

sent - verb; specifically a simple past verb which indicates that the person has already performed the given action.

the card - direct object; This is the thing which is being directly affected by the verb. Without the verb *send*, there is no *the card* in this statement; without the *the card*, there is nothing to be *sent* in this statement. You can test the veracity of this by trying to rewrite the sentence without the direct object. "I am sending."/"I send." Great. What is being sent exactly? Without a direct object, these sentences make no sense.

to her. - indirect object; This is the thing which is being indirectly affected by the verb and is the end recipient of the consequences of the action of the verb. That is to say that the *indirect* object is non-essential where the *direct* object is essential. If you're ever confused in a sentence as to which is which, the first thing you should do is look for a preposition - indirect objects are usually sitting after a "to" or "at". However, the other thing you can do is try to rewrite the sentence once for each object without including the other. (In your head, if you'd like - doing it in real life would be rather wasteful.) The one which makes the least sense is invariably the one wherein the direct object has been removed. Compare "I sent the card." to "I sent to her." The only times that the second structure are permissible are when it's an idiomatic structure wherein the direct object is heavily implied or otherwise unneeded (consider the Victorian-era idiomatic phrasal verb "to send for [somebody]" meaning "to summon [somebody]", which has its roots in sending somebody like a messenger to go and get the person in question).

In other words, you will know which is the direct object and which isn't by which one can be taken out without the sentence losing any and all practical meaning.

So how do we express these sorts of pronouns in English? Well, let's shift our focus to the direct object pronouns again.

The way that we express direct object pronouns are by the use of pronouns such as "*me*", "*it*", "*him*", "*them*", and so forth. Let's take that sentence again. "I sent the card to her." *Her* is a indirect object pronoun because it replaces the traditional indirect object of the sentence which would be the *person's name*.

This indeed also turns this into a discussion of when you would use direct objects; the answer is after establishing relevancy for them. If a person or thing is mentioned by you or somebody else in a sentence, and that becomes the subject of the conversation, then you can by all means start to use object pronouns as heavily as you wish. If you fail to have some sort of initial object concept presented either by you or somebody else, all you're going to do is sound a tad bit confused at best or a tad bit crazy at worst.

Pro

In English, if I wanted to make this sentence simpler though, I could. Relatively easily too. Since we say "I sent the card" instead of "a card", we can boldly assume that the topic of conversation has already been established to be about both the card and the girl in question. So we could simplify this by replacing "the card" with the relevant direct object pronoun which would here be "it". So the sentence could become "I sent it to her." Following so far?

Spanish treats this sort of thing in a rather simple way. The Spanish layout for verbs and objects is flipped though. Their format for this sort of thing is as follows:

(subject) (indirect object) (direct object) (verb)

This format is often referred to as *SIODOV*.

There are several different direct object pronouns in Spanish. Their general meaning is as such:

Direct Object Pronouns

Pronoun	Meaning
Me	Me
Te	You
Lo	Him or It depending upon context
La	Her or It depending upon context
Nos	Us
Os	You (plural)
Los/las	Them

And the indirect object pronouns are very similar. Their only real difference is the dropping of gender in the third person pronouns.

Indirect Object Pronouns

Pronoun	Meaning
Me	Me
Te	You
Le/se	Him, Her, or It depending upon context
Nos	Us

Os	You (plural)
Les/se	Them

So let's go back to our example sentence, "I sent the card to her." When we write this in Spanish, before taking into account the direct object, we're going to transform "to her" into an indirect object, like so:

I <u>sent</u> the card **to her**.

(Yo) **Le** <u>envié</u> la tarjeta.

Yo is in parentheses because in virtually all forms of spoken and written Spanish, you'd drop the subject pronoun. If you didn't, then you'd risk sounding like you have no idea what you're saying and likewise have no business speaking Spanish in the first place.

Now, we can convert "la tarjeta" into a direct object pronoun so we're saying what is the Spanish equivalent of "I sent her it." or "I sent it to her." Super simple but pretty involving.

Since *la tarjeta* is a feminine noun, we need to use the third person singular feminine direct object pronoun. This would of course be *la*. And according to the presented rules of the *SIODOV* protocol, we're going to smush that in between our indirect object pronoun and our verb. So our sentence would come out like this:

(Yo) **le** la <u>envié</u>.

So we went from a massive and bulky sentence to something that's rather elegant. (Provided you have the appropriate context to make sense of a vague statement like "I sent her it" or "Le la envié.")

That draws this lesson on pronouns to an end, I'm afraid.

Conclusion

Thank for making it through to the end of *Learn Spanish: A Fast and Easy Guide for Beginners to Learn Conversational Spanish*, let's hope it was informative and able to provide you with all of the tools you need to achieve your goals whatever they may be.

The next step is to build upon the knowledge you've procured. As I'm sure you've noticed, my intent in this book wasn't to flood you over with vocabulary words or make you memorize a million things. Rather, my sole intent was that you walk away understanding the mechanical foundations of Spanish impeccably well.

The beauty of language is that it's the fundamental crux of civilization. There is no way that we could have developed anywhere near as far as we have had we not had the ability to communicate via spoken and written language. Truly, language is one of the most beautiful things in the universe.

That's why I feel so honored to have been afforded the opportunity to help you to understand Spanish better as you learn and go forward with it. My sincere hope is that I've given you at the very least a solid foundation that you can build *on top* of, because I know that my pet peeve with language learning books are those that fail to teach certain things in depth and are effectively trying to build a brick house on a very shaky foundation of linguistic knowledge.

And to be quite frank with you, I don't feel like that approach works, either. Only practice and immersion can make somebody a better language learner.

If at any point going forward with learning Spanish or French or Chinese or whatever that you may learn in the future, you feel that you're unable to full carry out your potential, or you feel that you just have hit a wall and can't go any further, then for me, quit lying to yourself. Absolutely anybody can learn another language. It takes time and work and dedication, often a lot more than most people have, but there are people born into bilingualism and trilingualism constantly. Not only that, but those same kids will often go on to learn yet *another* language later in life.

I guess the point that I'm trying to make here in closing is that my teaching method is a tad unorthodox because my whole belief in language learning is that giving you a long list of vocabulary words to memorize isn't the way to go about it; I genuinely feel that the only way for you to improve is through constant and concentrated effort being actively put forth towards a given language, and exerting energy in the general direction of making yourself better.

If you wish to flesh out your vocabulary, the way I earnestly recommend doing it is going to http://wordreference.com/enes/ and http://spanishdict.com/conjugate/ and working as hard as you can. Start writing a private blog or journal in order to learn new words and phraseologies. And, if you do find yourself wishing for more vocabulary-centric learning, I highly recommend Duolingo.

Finally, if you found this book useful in anyway, a review on Amazon is always appreciated!

Help me improve this book

While I have never met you, if you made it through this book I know that you are the kind of person that is wanting to get better and is willing to take on tough feedback to get to that point. You and I are cut from the same cloth in that respect. I am always looking to get better and I wish to not just improve myself, but also this book. If you have positive feedback, please take the time to leave a review. It will help other find this book and it can help change a life in the same way that it changed yours. If you have constructive feedback, please also leave a review. It will help me better understand what you, the reader, need to make significant improvements in your life. I will take your feedback and use it to improve this book so that it can become more powerful and beneficial to all those who encounter it.

REMEMBER TO JOIN THE GROUP NOW!

If you have not joined the Mastermind Self Development group yet, now is your time! You will receive videos and articles from top authorities in self development as well as a special group only offers on new books and training programs. There will also be a monthly member only draw that gives you a chance to win any book from your Kindle wish list!

If you sign up through this link http://www.mastermindselfdevelopment.com/specialreport you will also get a special free report on the Wheel of Life. This report will give you a visual look at your current life and then take you through a series of exercises that will help you plan what your perfect life looks like. The workbook does not end there; we then take you through a process to help you plan how to achieve that perfect life. The process is very powerful and has the potential to change your life forever. Join the group now and start to change your life!
http://www.mastermindselfdevelopment.com/specialreport

You will also love these other great titles from Mastermind Self Development!

You will want to check out these other great titles Mastermind Self Development. All available in the Kindle store or you can just click on covers below.

http://getbook.at/AstrologyBeginner

http://getbook.at/Astrologyguide

You can also find these titles by searching them in the Kindle store on Amazon.

www.ingramcontent.com/pod-product-compliance
Lightning Source LLC
Chambersburg PA
CBHW081402070526
44583CB00020B/2638